It's almost nightfall.
The sun is gone in the sea;
The birds are crying.

When the waves break out,
The reef is as white as clouds.
Bubbles are floating.

Beyond the far reef
Where the sea is dark and blue,
The fish are jumping.
—SEBASTIAN SHIRO

Micronesia: Island Wilderness

Foreword

RISING ABOVE Micronesia's three million square miles of the Pacific are two thousand two hundred islands smaller in their aggregate area than Rhode Island, the American minimum. Small though the island wilderness is, it may hold a secret the developed world needs. It may show how the idea of a World Heritage, conceived by a conservationist and blessed by the United Nations, can be fully realized at last. The World Heritage would encompass scenic, cultural, and ecological resources of major importance to the world as a whole; all nations would share in sparing, for all future generations, the beauty and knowledge unique in these places.

To suggest what Micronesia's share of these places is like, Robert Wenkham and Kenneth Brower have collaborated—for a third time. (Their earlier books were on the Hawaiian islands of Kauai and Maui.) Mr. Wenkham's photography and writing of the Pacific basin have informed a wide and growing audience. Kenneth Brower has now had a key role in twelve volumes in the present format, eight for the Sierra Club and four for Friends of the Earth. They describe islands of diversity in various parts of the world, and the ingenuity with which varied peoples have adapted to that diversity without destroying it and themselves.

Kenneth Brower writes here of the people, and their cultural problems and conservation opportunities, as he saw them in two voyages in the islands. In his earlier *With Their Islands Around Them* (1974), he described the impact of the islands on two widely different men—one a veteran American conservation officer, the other his young half-Japanese, half-Palauan successor. In *Micronesia: Island Wilderness,* he looks at the broader stage:

"Other things being equal, it would seem that the civilization that displaces least water is best. But it has been decided, apparently, that this is not so: that the success of millennia is of no account and the island cultures that passed on, through all those successive generations, the living reefs and their various and variegated fishes, and the green fecund jungles, and the flawless beaches painfully white in the sun, must now give way to a civilization that can't pass a thing on intact, and has never learned to live harmoniously with anything. . . .

"Discovered late by the traders and colonizers of Asia, Europe, and America, the Micronesian wilderness is now entering the last quarter of the twentieth century largely intact, but there is a proliferation of omens that this may change."

One omen lies in a remark now well known to all literate Micronesians. When their need to own their own land was being urged by then Secretary of the Interior Walter Hickel, Henry Kissinger replied: "There are only 90,000 people out there. Who gives a damn?"

There are now 110,000 Micronesians who do, and we hope there will be millions of other people elsewhere. It is hard to tell from someone else's book just what Dr. Kissinger had in mind. Perhaps he alluded to the attitude shared by generals and admirals that the islands are strategic and the people aren't. Certainly no one who remembers the changing of the island guard in World War II will deny how strategic some of those islands were in the battle era, so technologically long ago.

Just as certainly, there are now better games that may here be played, and more Thoreauvian, hopeful attitudes to be brought to bear. One of the most hopeful is that there be a revised strategy for preserving what makes life possible on a small planet. The national-park idea is one strategy, and Friends of the Earth has proposed in several earlier books in this series that the idea evolve to include people who have lived long in equilibrium with the earth, who have treated it as if it were all an Earth National Park.

In his Preface, Raymond Dasmann, looking back on his years of contributions to international conservation, states powerfully the case for parks of a new kind in the Pacific. In their own introduction, Robert Wenkham and Kenneth Brower, after the kind of consultation with native islanders that Mr. Dasmann believes is essential, propose a system of such parks for one part of the Pacific, Micronesia. Theirs is a way to begin.

There is a way not to begin. For example, the U.S. Trust Territory government should not import U.S. National Park Service staffers from Honolulu, say, to compile a "federal" inventory of scenic and historical sites. They should not create a Historic Preservation Program and put an American in charge. The High Commissioner of the Trust Territory should not introduce a bill in the Congress of Micronesia that calls for the establishment of a "national" park system and outlines the procedures for acquisition of land for the purpose. The U.S. Department of the Interior should not unilaterally declare six sites within Micronesia in the "United States" National Register of Historic Places. All these things, unfortunately, have come to pass. There is no better way to sour Micronesians, or any people weary of imperialism, on the idea of parks.

Parks may be established at the fiat of the great powers in the Pacific, but they will not stay established. Neo-imperialism won't work in conservation any better than it has worked in other recent enterprises overendowed with benign arrogance, real neglect, no little greed, and almost malevolent disinterest.

For inhabitants do indeed give a damn. The people of Maap, an island in the Micronesian archipelago of Yap, have eloquently said so to the entire world, with special reference to Japan's multinational Nanyo Boeki Kaisha corporation. NBK had plans for a resort development on Maap. The corporation anticipated native opposition by camouflaging its intent behind a dummy euphemism, a firm called Yap Nature Life Garden Incorporated. It began development on a small scale, constructing no permanent buildings. The first Japanese guests lived in tents and ate from temporary kitchens. NBK's long-range plans, for forty-seven air-conditioned concrete block cottages, a five-hundred-foot pier extending to the barrier reef, and a swimming area dredged from the inner reef, were plans well hidden.

When the people of Maap found them out, most of the adult population signed a petition against NBK, a petition dictated by the chiefs of the island and translated by attorneys with the U.S. Office of Economic Opportunity in Colonia.

The petition was addressed to "legal, governmental, or other authorities or persons . . . within and beyond the district of Yap . . . and to all who love justice." In part it ran thus:

"Whereas we love our lands and the ways in which we live together there in peace, and yet live humbly and still cherish them above all other ways, and are not discontent to be the children of our fathers, it has become apparent to us that we have been persuaded to subscribe to processes that will quickly extinguish all that we hold dear.

"By usurping unnegotiated lands, assuming nearly dictatorial manners in the area where it operates, obscuring the nature and the extent of its ambitions and the inevitable and irreversible injury that these will cause to our customs and our pride, the company has far exceeded all pretense to legality and welcome to our land. It plans to make a dead sea of our lagoon, and thus a dead place of its shores.

"We, men and women of Maap of majority age, now urgently and passionately unite to repudiate and refuse all association with that company and to ask the help of the people, customary leaders and district officers of Yap, and legal, governmental and international bodies within and beyond the Trust Territory of the Pacific Islands in ridding us of this invasion and freeing us, that we do not become servants in our own land."

The chiefs of Maap then adopted a resolution:

"We, pilungs and langanpagels, elders and elected officers, Chiefs in Council of and on behalf of all the people of the Eighteen Villages and Fiefs of the Island of Maap . . . declare our love of this place and of the ways passed down to us by the generations. We have inherited from our fathers a land that is lovely and provides for us with the fruits of the earth and of the sea. We are few in numbers but have a brave history and are strong in our resolve to preserve these things that are sweet to us.

"Henceforth any proposal, from whomsoever it may come, be it even one of us, that threatens by change or innovation to infringe upon the integrity of our well-loved ways or of the land and the waters about us that have so long sustained them, should be first submitted . . . for review and evaluation.

"We meet today under the shadow of such change and innovation and we know our people to be roused against such things, as they today do forcefully convey through petition. We are therefore all the more solemnly moved to affirm our united will in the face of the unfamiliar contingencies of this age and the ages to come. . . ."

Unfamiliar contingencies are likely to be common in Micronesia in the future. In Palau, the archipelago south of Yap, the American military plans to place a training base for jungle warfare, with old expansionist-day overtones. The Japanese plan an enormous oil-storage facility for the supertankers that speed the spilling and exhaustion of oil. The drive for mindless growth that nourishes such developments means the extinction of cultures that remember what balance means to well-being. The Palauans, who are resisting these designs on their country, will need great courage to continue to do so, in the face of rapaciousness from East and West. If they lose, we all lose.

Micronesians cannot defend themselves against the great powers who now seek to make the islands of Micronesia something else and something less. It is the powers themselves who must learn what the unique island beauty means to the eye and ear, and to the conscience.

San Francisco
May 9, 1975

DAVID R. BROWER, *President*
Friends of the Earth, International

Parks, Nature Conservation, and "Future Primitive"

IT IS LITTLE wonder that those concerned with conservation of nature in America attempted to set some areas aside, and it is remarkable that they were as successful as they were in doing so. But is there not cause to wonder that it was accepted that those lands outside the national parks were going to be beaten and battered, or used in such a way that any hope for the survival of wildlife in their vicinity was to be considered an idle dream? Is it not strange that it was taken for granted that people and nature were somehow incompatible, and that the drive for profit or power must take precedence over any concern for the kind of world in which people live? People were not always that way. Perhaps it would be well to listen to Chief Standing Bear of the Oglala Sioux (known in his day as the Lakotas):

"The old Lakota was wise. He knew that man's heart away from nature becomes hard; he knew that lack of respect for growing, living things soon led to lack of respect for humans too. So he kept his youth close to its softening influence."

I recently postulated that there are two types of people in the world, *ecosystem people* and *biosphere people*. In the former category are all of the members of indigenous traditional cultures and some who have seceded from, or have been pushed out of, technological society; in the latter are those who are tied in with the global technological civilization. Ecosystem people live within a single ecosystem, or at most two or three adjacent and closely related ecosystems. They are dependent upon that ecosystem for their survival. If they persistently violate its ecological rules, they must necessarily perish. Thus a hunting people who continually kill more wild game than can be produced by the normal reproduction of wild animal populations must run out of food and starve. A fishing people who persist in overfishing will destroy their base of support. Those who practice subsistence agriculture must develop some means for keeping the soil in place and for restoring its fertility. Island people have lived under particularly strong restraints, and could not tolerate any great increase in their own numbers, since the resources of islands are not only limited but tend to make their limitations obvious. Only continental people can develop myths of unlimited resources.

Biosphere people draw their support, not from the resources of any one ecosystem, but from the entire biosphere. Any large modern city is the focus for a network of transportation and communication that reaches throughout the globe—drawing perhaps beef from Argentina, lamb from New Zealand, wheat from Canada, tea from Ceylon, coffee from Brazil, herring from the North Atlantic, and so on. Local catastrophes that would wipe out people dependent on a single ecosystem may create only minor perturbations among the biosphere people, since they can simply draw more heavily on a different ecosystem. Consequently, biosphere people can exert incredible pressure upon an ecosystem that they wish to exploit, and create great devastation—something that would be impossible or unthinkable for people who were dependent upon that particular ecosystem. The impact of biosphere people upon ecosystem people has usually been destructive. Even if the intentions of the biosphere invaders are the best, and they seldom are, their effect is to break down the local constraints, the traditional practices that have held the delicate balances between humanity and nature, and thus allow ecosystem destruction to take place.

In the Pacific we see some glaring examples of what happens when ecosystem peoples are brought into the biosphere network. The people of Nauru would never have thought of mining their island out from under themselves, until they were tied into the trade and transportation of the biosphere network. The same applies to other phosphate islands. No ecosystem person would have thought of taking the top off New Caledonia to get at the nickel, until he was sucked into the biosphere network.

Biosphere people create national parks. Ecosystem people have always lived in the equivalent of a national park. It is the kind of country that ecosystem people have always protected that biosphere people want to have formally reserved and safeguarded. But, of course, first the ecosystem people must be removed—or at least that has been the prevailing custom. The consequences are almost always destructive to the people affected. Colin Turnbull's book *The Mountain People* is a particularly disturbing account of what happened to a hunting-subsistence-agriculture people when they were pushed out of Uganda's Kidepo Valley National Park.

It is a characteristic of wealthier biosphere people that they do not want to stay at home. They wander the globe always searching—searching for something they seem to have lost along the way in their rush to capture the resources of the world and accumulate its wealth. Thus they give rise to the tourist industry, and this in turn provides a financial justification for creating and maintaining national parks. In these parks the wanderers can see some of the wonders that they left behind, and can pretend for a while that they have not really destroyed the natural world—at least not all of it. They will pay highly for this experience. But for some reason the money nearly always tends to be channelled back into this biosphere network. It does not go to those who were once ecosystem people and who have the strange idea that what is now called a national park is really just the land that was home.

This situation must not continue. National parks must not serve as a means for displacing the members of traditional societies who have always cared for the land and its biota. Nor can national parks survive as islands surrounded by hostile people who have lost the land that was once their home. Parks cannot survive in a natural state if they are surrounded by lands that are degraded or devastated by failure to obey the simplest ecological rules. Today, with the increase in human numbers and the enormous pressure being exerted on all ecosystems, one of the distinctions between ecosystem and total biosphere is being broken down. No longer can biosphere people remain buffered against the breakdown of particular ecosystems. A drought in India or North America now has global repercussions. The entire biosphere is now becoming as close interconnected through human endeavor as the most delicately balanced ecosystem within it. Not just national parks but nature conservation in its fullest sense are now becoming absolutely vital.

In the South Pacific there is no doubt that more national parks, or something equivalent to them, are badly needed. There is some question, however, about what kind of national park, and how it is to fit in with the patterns of life, and the necessities of life, for those people who inhabit the Pacific. I would suggest that the ideal national park for the Pacific islands would be fairly close to what existed here before the invaders from Europe and Asia took over. I do not propose, however, that we attempt to turn back the clock. I am suggesting, however, that in going forward we take into account some rules that should be mandatory for those agencies, national or international, responsible for advocating or creating new national parks.

1. The rights of members of indigenous cultures to the lands they have traditionally occupied must be recognized, and any plans for establishing parks or reserves in these lands must be developed in consultation with, and in agreement with, the people involved. Papua/New Guinea has been taking some noteworthy initiatives in this direction, and I trust that their government will continue along this course. Furthermore, the Australian government has now fully recognized the rights of its Aborigines to their lands, including mineral rights.

2. Recognizing the long-prevailing balances that have existed between people and nature in areas where traditional societies have remained isolated from the influence of biosphere cultures, the establishment of fully protected areas in which these people can maintain their isolation *for so long as they wish to do so* should be encouraged. Such areas will do much to further the conservation of nature, and equally important will protect ways-of-life that are in balance with nature. We all have much to learn from these traditional cultures. In this respect there are some examples to follow. The Manu National Park in Peru shelters an isolated Indian tribe which, for the present at least, remains undisturbed. The Odzala National Park in the Congo provides a home for pygmy people. In Botswana and South Africa the 6 million hectares of the Central Kalahari Game Reserve and Kalahari Gemsbok National Parks permit the Bushmen to continue their traditional hunting life.

3. Wherever national parks are created, their protection needs to be coordinated with the people who occupy the surrounding lands. Those who are most affected by the presence of a national park must fully share in its benefits, financial or other. They must become the protectors of the park, whether they are directly employed by the park, receive a share of park receipts, or are in other ways brought to appreciate its value. Without this, we will find that we are entering a waiting game, at best. The people outside the park will await the change in government or the relaxation of vigilance that will permit them to invade the park.

4. Land use in areas surrounding parks must be compatible with the protection of nature inside the park. This too will require negotiation and understanding among the people who own or occupy these lands. It cannot be effectively accomplished by some sweeping government decree unless the lands are unoccupied.

I would propose that the answer for nature conservation in the South Pacific, as elsewhere, will be found to lie in the direction of "Future Primitive." This does not mean the rejection of the best of modern technology, but it does mean the avoidance of the worst. It does mean using the tools and energy that are still available to create something permanent, to create a way of life that can be *sustained*. In such a way of life, nature conservation would necessarily be taken for granted, since people will recognize that their future depends on the health and diversity of the natural world.

—RAYMOND FREDRIC DASMANN

Wellington, New Zealand
February 1975

Such is the nature of the ocean that the waters which flow into it can never fill it, nor those which flow from it exhaust it.

CHUANG TZU
369-286 B.C.

by Kenneth Brower

photographs and an introduction by

Robert Wenkam

Prefatory statements by

David R. Brower and Raymond F. Dasmann

Micronesia: Island Wilderness

FRIENDS OF THE EARTH ✦ SAN FRANCISCO, NEW YORK, LONDON, PARIS

A CONTINUUM BOOK / THE SEABURY PRESS NEW YORK

THE EARTH'S WILD PLACES
PUBLISHER'S NOTE AND ACKNOWLEDGMENTS

THE NAME for the series, "The Earth's Wild Places," comes from Loren Eiseley's introduction to the prologue to the series, the two-volume *Galapagos: The Flow of Wildness*. The series was initiated in 1968 by its general editor, David Brower, while he was with the Sierra Club, and has been continued by Friends of the Earth, founded in 1969. The idea of the series was born in 1963. John P. Milton had a key role. Dr. Harold Coolidge, a moving force in international conservation, assisted, as did Russell Train. Major assistance in the launching came from Eliot Porter, one of the world's great photographers. Several people in the Sierra Club's publishing program gave invaluable help, and a most generous, anonymous donor made the beginning in the Galapagos financially feasible.

The editor and principal author of the first two volumes—and a principal in five of the eight that have followed—was Kenneth Brower. In *Galapagos*, agreeing with Loren Eiseley that "voyages without islands to touch upon would be epics of monotony," Kenneth Brower suggested the kind of voyage the series itself is embarked upon:

"The book arose from concern for islands and the fragile forms they have evolved, the gentle insular wildness that is vanishing so rapidly around the world. Its concern is both for oceanic islands like the Galapagos, and for islands isolated in other ways—for islands of life, like the very small North American island of whooping cranes, a last island of common genes and nesting calls, or like the limited fraternity of the Indian rhinoceros, or that of the fresh-water seals of Lake Baikal. Its plea is for diversity, for all possible variety, animate and inanimate, in the texture of our planet's surface. . . .

"We don't need more emptiness in the world—there is presently a surfeit of that. We need to celebrate the opposite of emptiness, and this series will attempt to do this, to point out the fullness and the variousness of the earth's wild places.

"A living planet is a rare thing, perhaps the rarest in the universe, and a very tenable experiment at best. We need all the company we can get on our unlikely journey. If an island is washed away mankind is the less: One species' death diminishes us, for we are involved in life. The more varied the life, the better. There is no requirement that our voyage be a monotonous one."

Two other organizations materially helped the scope grow—the Conservation Foundation and the Nature Conservancy. John Milton and Dr. Maria Buchinger, respectively concerned with the international programs of these organizations, described a threat few people were aware of when the series began:

"Greatly expanded efforts will be needed to counteract successfully the adverse effects of much of our country's massive governmental and private 'development' programs throughout the world. We hope more North Americans will take heed of environmental problems in developing nations. At best this will lead to an accelerated support of local conservation activities. . . . Moreover, in the excitement of watching our own technology change the face of our part of the Americas, we have overlooked some important lessons abroad. Those who have already worked out an enduring relationship with the land have much to teach us."

The purpose of the series was also seen clearly by Jerry Mander, who in a famous Sierra Club advertisement said that the series would advance an urgent idea—"An international program, before it is too late, to preserve Earth as a 'conservation district within the Universe': a sort of 'Earth National Park.'" Mr. Mander shortly thereafter visited Micronesian islands and reported his findings to a 1969 Aspen conference. These places, he said, could teach all the world about "the islandness of things." None of the islands is very large—many of them may be walked around in an hour or two—and it makes them no bigger and no more beautiful to walk around them faster.

The series has initiated many voyages: by Robert Wenkam, camera and notebook in hand, around the Pacific Basin; by Kenneth Brower, to the Galapagos Islands, to Kauai and Maui, to Borneo, to several islands of the Micronesian group, and to a very special kind of island, one of a very old culture, near the Brooks Range of Alaska. His voyages also took him to tinier islands still—to the paragraphs that islands had led many people to write about over a long time— Homer, Shakespeare, Dampier, Melville, Defoe, Darwin, Mark Twain, Robert Louis Stevenson, Louise Dickinson Rich, and others too, whose writings have influenced Kenneth Brower. Not only to the Micronesian children quoted here, but also to all Micronesians who helped we are grateful, especially to Lynn Grohman, Robert Owen, Singer Kochi, Ronn Ronck, and Roger Gale. We wish we knew that all the people in the long roster agreed about what now should happen to Micronesia, but it is not given to people to agree too long about anything, and we shall have to defer asking some of them until later. We can hope, however, that Micronesia will always remain the essential part of Earth National Park it already is, that it will be beautiful and enduringly so, and that the world, all of it, will heed what Robert Wenkam sent to us in press—the exquisite statement that follows from the people of Maap, an island in the Micronesian archipelago of Yap.

*   *   *

We acknowledge with thanks the co-publishing coöperation the series has enjoyed successively with the John Muir Institute for Environmental Studies, the McCall Publishing Company, Saturday Review Press, Ballantine Books, Allen and Unwin, Earth Island, and The Seabury Press. The principal firms responsible for the excellence of the graphic arts have been Mackenzie & Harris, Inc., San Francisco; Carl DeSchutter, Antwerp; Barnes Press, New York; H. S. Crocker, San Francisco; Garrod and Lofthouse, London; Edita s a, Lausanne; and Mondadori Editore, Verona. The people of Mondadori have had a hand in producing seven of the ten titles, and we are grateful for the craftsmanship of all the people, who in addition to other duties have welcomed the visits, from an island just off Europe, of Philip Evans. He, in behalf of Friends of the Earth, has looked over Mondadori shoulders as the presses roll. We mention in particular Mondadori's Roberto Voltolina, who has served as Mr. Evans' interpreter for so long that his Italian now has a Welsh accent.

We add our aggregate gratitude to many publishers for their kindness through the years in letting us reprint small facets of gems they discovered in the first place. We are grateful for permission to reprint herein excerpts from the following books:

Charles Scribner's Sons, New York: *The Night Country*, by Loren Eiseley, 1971.

Sierra Club, San Francisco: *Galapagos: The Flow of Wildness*, edited by Kenneth Brower, 1968.

University of Washington Press: *Flower in My Ear: Arts and Ethos of Ifaluk Atoll*, by Edwin Grant Burrows, 1963.

Published in New York by Friends of the Earth, Inc., and simultaneously in Paris by Les Amis de la Terre and in London by Friends of the Earth Ltd.

Library of Congress Catalog Card No. 73-80332

ISBN: 0-913890-13-8.

Lithographed and bound in Italy.

SIXTY-ONE COLOR PLATES

INTRODUCTION

Toward Oceanic Parks for Micronesia—a Proposal

THE 2,203 islands of Micronesia are scattered over three million square miles of ocean. The combined land area of the region is less than that of Rhode Island, yet, in its separation by vast stretches of ocean, the land is vastly diverse, geologically, biologically, and culturally. There are both "high" islands—volcanically active in the Marianas, extinct in Palau, Yap, Truk, and Ponape—and "low" islands, the atolls of the Yap and Truk districts and the Marshalls. The human inhabitants live on a scattered ninety islands, of which some are occupied only by a single family, or by a seasonal copra-harvesting party. The rest of the islands are wilderness. With a few exceptions, even the inhabited islands are wild, for the traditional life is not the kind that makes land tame.

Discovered late by the traders and colonizers of Asia, Europe, and America, the Micronesian wilderness, in a manner reprieved, is now entering the last third of the twentieth century largely intact, but there is a recent proliferation of omens that this may change. Here and there in the Trust Territory of the Pacific Islands, as most of Micronesia is politically designated, colonial bureaucrats are at work, stripping a unique beach of its sand for construction, or flattening an entire island to make a jet field, or commissioning feasibility studies for phosphate strip-mining and reef dredging for pink coral. The American military has a substantial presence here. Ten years after the Marshallese atoll of Kwajalein was captured from the Japanese, it was transformed into an ABM missile test facility. Today missiles from Kwajalein intercept missiles fired from southern California, and the Marshalls, the gentlest of Micronesia's islands, is practice ground for war.

The potential that tourism holds for the destruction of the traditional life of the islands is great. Increasing numbers of tourists are arriving: Americans flying westward, escaping Hawaii, where Tourism has Tropical Charm down and is twisting its arm; and Japanese flying south from Tokyo and Okinawa. Guam is now a favorite spot for Japanese honeymooners, and certain of the other islands, all of which were ruled by Japan a generation ago under a League of Nations mandate, are now being redis-

covered. Tourist dollars are only beginning to trickle in, yet a reaction by Micronesians has begun. The residents of the Yapese island of Rumung, shocked by the behavior of their first American tourists, have declared the island off-limits, and have been supported in this by the Yapese Legislature. The Ponape Legislature voted unanimously to ask the High Commissioner of the Trust Territory to forbid an American company from building a hotel

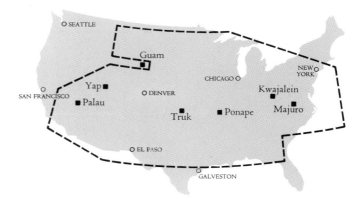

on Ponape. On the back streets of Koror, teenage Palauan boys stone white visitors. Palau and other Micronesian districts are experiencing problems with juvenile delinquency, a phenomenon the islands never knew before.

The toxicity of certain fish is a natural phenomenon in coral seas. It's an old paradox: certain species of reef fish have always been as deadly to eat as they are beautiful. But of late, this toxicity has been increasing. In the Bikini lagoon, where before the H-bomb only a few varieties of toxic fish lived, there are now many species never poisonous before. Or so say the Bikini chiefs who recently visited their former home.

None of these changes has been more ominous than the invasion of *Acanthaster planci*, the crown-of-thorns starfish. Until the early 1960's, this many-armed, poison-spined echinoderm was a rare inhabitant of the coral, its population in balance with the myriad other reef species. The adult starfish ate coral, and the coral ate the larval starfish—a short and healthy cycle. The first evidence that something was wrong came in 1962. In that year, Typhoon Karen's 160 mile-per-hour winds struck Guam, tearing up tons of coral and tossing it on the island's beaches. Through rents in the protective reef, high seas immediately began eroding Guam's shore.

Coral, when it is alive, resists the heaviest seas—it is designed for that. The typhoon's uprooting it revealed that Guam's coral was dying. After the storm, skin divers went out, and discovered a ghost reef for miles around Tumon Bay. They found that forty per cent of the coral surrounding Guam was dead; twenty-four miles of living reef destroyed. The associations of small fish that normally live in the coral were gone. The coral was reduced to a colorless, crumbling chalk. The live coral that remained was swarming with starfish. The giant (two feet across), sixteen-armed creatures flowed along the reef, their movement like a slow and inexorable forest fire. They migrated at the rate of half a mile each month, feeding as they went by everting their stomachs, as starfish do, and ingesting, directly through the stomach wall, the living matter of the coral—the thousands of individual animals, polyps, that manufacture and occupy each rocky coral branch. Where the starfish had grazed, the coral was first a bone-white. In time a dull ooze enshrouded it. Where bright coral colors had clashed in all their variety, there was now a monotone.

Whether the explosion of starfish numbers was due to human disturbance of the reef ecosystem, perhaps through dredging (coral that is killed by dredging makes ideal breeding ground for starfish), or through shell-collecting (the triton mollusk, a favorite of collectors, is a predator on the adult starfish), or weapons testing, or as a delayed consequence of the war in the Pacific, or a combination of these; or whether—though this seems less likely—the explosion was natural, part of a very long cycle, is unknown. But under the starfish onslaught the islands might have disappeared from the face of the deep. When the reef is gone, there is nothing to keep the ocean out. Just as the beach at Guam eroded, so conceivably could have entire archipelagos. There would be no one to watch the last peak slip under, of course, for the island people, dependent as they are on the creatures of a living reef, would have long since departed.

For several years the starfish multiplied out of all control. The explosion was a better subject for science fiction than natural history—an invasion of the sort that comes only from outer space in movies; a starfish from the stars. When a diver cut *Acanthaster* in two, the halves would regenerate and the starfish, like a monster in myth, was duplicated. But Micronesian schoolchildren were put to work picking starfish from the reef and bringing them ashore to die in the sun. Scuba teams were organized in every district of the Trust Territory to kill the starfish of deeper waters. The divers injected the starfish with an ammonia solution, and the starfish disintegrated. These efforts, aided perhaps by a defensive reaction of the ecosystem itself, were successful. The crown-of-thorns is under control in Micronesia. The starfish were not the agents of extinction, it turns out, but a warning, like mineshaft canaries. The warning was likely a major one, of the order that Noah heeded.

For these, and the other problems that have taken shape on Micronesia's horizon, a system of Oceanic Parks might serve as a first line of defense. To be effective as such, the park system would need be ambitious. Park boundaries could not end at the shoreline. They would have to extend beyond, into the undersea wilderness of lagoon and reef without which the bits of land above water would be uninhabitable and incomplete. The parks could not be simply scenic reserves. Many of the islands, the atolls especially, are just palmed and sandy rafts that require people for substance, so the parks need also be reservoirs of Micronesian tradition, of Micronesian humanity. To be effective, the park system will have to be innovative. The U.S. National Park System can provide hints, but a Micronesian system that is purely imitative will fail. On many islands, for example, ownership would probably best remain with chiefs and villages, to be leased to the park system, which would provide maintenance, protection, and interpretation. Concessions would be run by the municipalities.

The details of Oceanic Park management and boundaries will have to be worked out by the Congress of Micronesia and its committees. Perhaps even "Oceanic" is wrong, and a better word needed. But a general scheme suggests itself. The park system should include all sites of scenic, historic, scientific, and recreational significance, both above and below the sea, in all districts of Micronesia. Smaller parks could be established by district legislatures and municipalities. These parks would remain under the jurisdiction of local officials. Marine sanctuaries, wildlife refuges, and forest reserves would also be established, both inside and outside park boundaries, in places where ecological circumstances require specialized management of land or sea. These areas would properly be placed under the jurisdiction of a Commission of Natural Resources, Fish and Wildlife appointed by the Congress of Micronesia.

These foregoing ideas for a Micronesian park system, necessarily sketchy now, and the list of proposed parks that follows, cannot be credited to any one source. They were developed in conversation and in correspondence between Friends of the Earth and Micronesians of every district. The proposal originated with Micronesians, and is in essence a plea to their elected representatives—the Congress of Micronesia—to save a unique terrain and way of life. We must acknowledge the contributions of Senators Amata Kabua, Tosiwo Nakayama, and Olympio Borja; District Administrators Francisco Ada, Oscar deBrum, Thomas Remengesau, Boyd MacKenzie, Juan Sablan, and Leonard Aguigui; Jonas Olkeriil, Pensile Lawrence, the Nahnmwarki of Madolenihmw; and the many other Micronesian officials and citizens whose ideas are here assembled.

The Oceanic Parks should be, foremost, parks by and for the Micronesian people. If they succeed in this, they will serve everyone else in the world. Amata Kabua, the President of the Senate of the Congress of Micronesia, sees an oceanic system of "parks for mankind." He envisions the whole of Micronesia as a vast international peace park for Earth. In a curious, sunny and daydream way, Micronesia—the islands and the idea of them—have always been that. The senator would make it official.

Nan Madol Oceanic Park

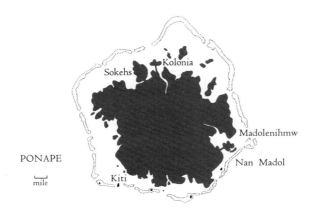

The European historian has a way of defining his own tradition into predominance. "Polynesia produced no Dante, Michelangelo, Shakespeare, Newton, or Goethe," writes Kenneth Clark, his observation true enough, as far as it goes. "The very fragility of those Arcadian societies—" Clark continues, in reference to the Pacific cultures, "the speed and completeness with which they collapsed on the peaceful appearance of a few British sailors followed by a handful of missionaries—shows that they were not civilisations . . ." It is hard to imagine a theory more thoroughly ungrounded in fact. The collapse Clark imagines was not complete (Arcadian societies endure in the Pacific, with diminished grandeur, but otherwise little changed), nor was the British appearance peaceful (British warships shelled the natives of the Palau Islands when they resisted exploitation by British traders, the Germans

behaved similarly in Ponape, as did the Japanese and Spanish elsewhere in Micronesia; and the French presently are detonating hydrogen bombs in Polynesia). Clark forgets that his few British sailors were accompanied by legions of microbes—spirochetes, gonococci, and viruses—and it was these tiny allies who accomplished the decimation of island populations and the decline of island society. The Britons were mucopurulent, unclean. A civilization that effects its superiority through venereal disease is not very civilized. If Clark is right about what makes "civilization" then perhaps a new definition is in order, or a new civilization. Clark forgets also that the Arcadian societies of the Pacific had, and have, a strange way of assimilating members of his own society. In the islands the conqueror often winds up conquered. One of the first Europeans to visit the Palau archipelago was an Englishman named Davis. Of Davis a later visitor wrote, "No remembrance of his original home or of the main traits of European culture remained with him. A very scanty knowledge of English was all this strange man had left. At the beginning of our acquaintance I often sought an opportunity to ask Mr. Davis for an explanation of this peculiar attitude, but weeks passed before I succeeded.

"'I don't want to know anything about England, Sir,' he said crossly. 'I live here satisfied and happy—fish in the water, taro in the ground, coconuts on the trees, warm sun and blue sky—enough for a man.'"

But even in Kenneth Clark's terms Micronesia had its civilization. The city of Nan Madol, in Ponape, had a Venetian gridwork of canals that an Othello, or any of Clark's Renaissance men, would have felt at home in. Nan Madol's temple city has fallen to ruins fit for the musings of a Hamlet, or of a British historian.

The Pacific peoples apparently were the first to build vessels capable of ocean travel over great distances. While Europeans were still rowing, Southeast Asians were sailing with fore-and-aft rigged sail and centerboard, relying on the same aerodynamic principle of lift as modern aircraft. There is evidence that Asian peoples, in vessels rigged thus, began the migrations that settled the Pacific islands as long ago as two to three thousand years before Christ. Their accomplishments in navigation and logistics then surpassed in certain respects those of Magellan and Cook, ages later. The European explorers returned with notes and flower samples: Pacific peoples set out with complete family groups, with seeds for food plants and for new civilizations.

These men who settled the Pacific were architects, politicians, and master navigators. They developed an extraordinary knowledge of the ocean and sky and applied it to maritime skills. Astronomical systems were developed locally, and were designed to guide navigation, not agriculture as in most places. (Seasons, in the tropics, have less effect on plants than on sailing canoes.) In his history of the Pacific Basin, Herman Friis writes of Micronesian navigation that, "A far-flung network of interisland exchange and refinement of knowledge bore fruit in the development of a rudimentary science, a definite international system . . . Only the European impact interrupted a spreading process whereby sidereal and lunar months were being coordinated."

The routes of early migration, over thousands of years and millions of miles, are untraceable, but it is likely that the Palau Islands were occupied first, Yap and the Marianas shortly afterward. The easternmost atolls of Micronesia, the Marshall Islands, were probably settled through the Gilbert Island and Ocean Island chains, themselves earlier settled by travelers from Fiji and Samoa. The high volcanic islands of the Eastern Carolines—Truk and Ponape—were likely colonized by Malayo-Polynesian voyagers who had sailed north from Indonesia by way of New Guinea and the New Hebrides.

The mainstream of Pacific migration departed from Southeast Asia. Did there remain in Micronesians a conciousness of the ancestral continent? Roland Force, Director of the Bishop Museum, believes that Palauans were aware at least of Indonesia and the Philippines, for, he says, "countless waves of migration must have ebbed and flowed through this aperture to the farther reaches of Oceania." Perhaps all Micronesians felt the distant mainland behind them. Island empires and clan systems may have been modeled on the sultanates of Asia. Cambodian temples may have been prototypes for the reef city at Nan Madol. But maybe not.

An oral account of the construction of Nan Madol has come down to us. Literate peoples have a habit of dismissing such unwritten history as legend, a habit we will avoid here:

Nan Madol was conceived and built by two brothers, Olsihpa and Olsohpa. The pair were high chiefs who designed the place as a center of government and worship. They began work at other sites, first near Sokehs on the north shore and later at Nankopworemen, but rough seas made these localities untenable. (It was necessary that the building materials be transported by water.) Finally a good site, accessible by water yet protected from high winter seas, was discovered on the reef off Temwen Island. A section of shallow reef, about a square mile and awash at high tide, was laid out into canals. Between these,

islands were built, and on them dwellings, temples, burial grounds, public areas, and forts were erected. In Ponapean *madol* means "spaces," and *Nan Madol* "Place of the Spaces" or "At the Spaces."

The city was built of many-faceted black columnar basalt blocks. The blocks were natural prisms, so they did not require carving, but some weighed five tons. They were transported to the Temwen Island reef from distant quarries, probably slung underwater beneath oversized log rafts. From the water they may have been rolled up ramps of crushed coral, the coral afterward used as fill for more artificial islands. The city was a tremendous undertaking for hand labor alone, and the project proved too ambitious for Olsihpa's and Olsohpa's subjects, without aid. All the people of Madolenihmw, the neighboring district, were recruited as laborers, and then most of the population of Ponape, and perhaps eventually even conscriptees from other islands of the Eastern Carolines.

The two brothers ruled Ponape from the completed city. After the death of Olsihpa, his brother Olsohpa ruled alone, assuming the title of Saudeleur. In time an orderly system of succession to Saudeleur was established. Sixteen Saudeleurs are known to have reigned with absolute power over all Ponape.

Carole Jencks, a Peace Corps Volunteer on Ponape, has recorded the names of those Saudeleurs who live most clearly in the memories of the people. *Mwohn Mwei* was the Saudeleur who succeeded Olsohpa. *Nenen Mwei* ruled through what is called "The Very Good Period," and during his reign he built a high respect for the aristocracy among the common people. *Sakone Mwei*'s reign is remembered as "The Period of Cruelty." Sakone is said to have decreed a death sentence for anyone who ate head lice, his favorite delicacy, instead of rendering them to the Saudeleur. *Raipwenleng* is remembered for his magical powers; *Saraiden Sapw* for his accumulation of great wealth and for beginning the custom whereby the Saudeleur was brought the first-ripened fruits of the island; *Raipwenlako* for his cannabalism; and *Ketiparelong* for committing suicide.

The last Saudeleur was *Saudemwohi*, whose history has come down to us laced with myth. Saudemwohi, the story goes, suspected the thunder god, Nahnsapwe, of an affair with his wife. The Saudeleur planned to capture the god and torture him to death on Pahn Kadira, the three-acre island that was administrative center for Nan Madol. Nahnsapwe escaped to Kusaie Island, four hundred miles to the southwest. On Kusaie the god found a woman of his own clan, and asked that she bear a son to avenge him. When the woman protested that she was too old, Nahnsapwe squeezed a lime into her eyes and she became in-

stantly pregnant. She bore a son, Isokelekel, who in time became a great warrior.

When Isokelekel felt he was ready, he gathered 333 warriors and sailed to Ponape. He arrived at Nan Madol posing as a visitor. He and his men were assigned quarters in the servants' island of Kelepwel, across the canal from Pahn Kadira. They quickly precipitated a quarrel, and in the ensuing fight drove the Saudeleur's men from Nan Madol. The warfare continued on the main island, where the Saudeleur was finally killed. Isokelekel assumed control of Ponape, and established a new succession of rulers, the Nahnmwarkis.

There have been twenty-one Nahnmwarkis, and Carole Jencks has recorded the most influential: *Isokelekel* ruled Ponape until the day he looked in a reflecting pool, saw his gray hair and aged body, despaired, and took his own life. His nephew, *Luhk en Mwei Maur,* ruled next. This Nahnmwarki and his son argued, and the son departed to become the first Nahnmwarki of Uh. *Luhk en Weid* is remembered for murdering his son, and *Luhk en Ned* for having thirty wives.

Nahnmwarki Paul ruled from 1872 to 1896. In the beginning of his reign, Paul's policy was to shoot all Christians on sight. Then one day he fired three shots at a Christian reading a bible in a canoe, missed them all, and was converted on the spot. He became a fine Christian. It is said that a revolt he led against the Spanish was successful because of his many prayers. Nahnmwarki *Moses Hadley* was one of the great grandchildren of Jim Hadley, who came to Ponape on an American whaler. Moses died in 1966 after thirty-five years as Nahnmwarki, the longest reign of all. Nahnmwarki *Samuel Hadley,* brother of Moses, succeeded him and is the present Nahnmwarki. He lives on Temwen Island at the channel entrance to Nan Dowas, the largest temple of Nan Madol. Visitors to Nan Madol who do not personally ask the Nahnmwarki's permission to enter the temple city may pay their respects by remaining seated in their boats while in sight of his residence.

In the early 1800's a great typhoon forced Nahnmwarki Luhk en Mallada to vacate the reef capital, and Nan Madol has not been inhabited since. (The temple city was always a symbol of Ponape's affluence and well-being: it was from the surplus of the larger island that Nan Madol lived, for besides some coconut, breadfruit, and banana trees, the sandy soil of the artificial islands did not provide enough for the rulers' large retinues. Smallpox and other European diseases so decimated Ponape's population that maintenance of the reef community became im-

possible, and none of the succeeding Nahnmwarkis was able to return.)

In the first century after abandonment, typhoons and tropical storms broke down the stone dikes on the ocean side of the city, and silted in its canals. Unobstructed waves swept inland, undermining the temple foundations. Breadfruit trees and coconut palms split canal revetments, and mangrove thickets overgrew burial grounds and places of worship. Vines covered walls a thousand years old. Nan Madol was entirely overgrown by jungle when German administrators—it was Germany's turn to govern Ponape in the early twentieth century—heard of a "phantom city" on the reef. German archaeologists made a partial excavation of the city in 1907. Ponapeans warned the scientists not to disturb the bones of buried royalty, but Governor Berg persisted in digging personally in the old tombs. One night the governor was kept awake by odd sounds from Temwen Island. The next day he was dead. The curse of the Nahnmwarkis is, apparently, as potent as that of the Pharaohs.

Nan Madol Oceanic Park would arrest the further decay of the canal city, a prospect that pleases the present Nahnmwarki. (Today there are no funds for maintenance, and stones continue to tumble.) The Park and its city would serve as a reminder, for those who need the cold weight and stony echo of megaliths, that civilization reached these waters before men with white skin.

Ponape has a number of other fine potential parks. *Madolenihmw District Park* would encompass the great bay of Madolenihmw, near Nan Madol, and would include the Retao River, and the forty-foot high Tunihren Parau (waterfall) in Kepirohi, and surrounding scenic lands. The park's primary purpose would be recreation: small boating, water skiing, hiking, picnics, camping, and in these things would complement the historical tours of adjacent Nan Madol. *Savertik District Park* would protect the two-hundred-foot Savertik falls in Salapwuk, Kiti, along with the smaller falls nearby, and Salapwuk gorge. A *Kolonia Municipal Park* for recreation would lie southeast of Kolonia Town on the scenic Doweneu River, and a complementary historical park in downtown Kolonia would preserve the old Spanish wall, the German church tower and cemetery, the graves of the Sokehs rebels, and the Kubary monument. Several historical sites, small places, yet important to Ponape's history, also suggest themselves: the ancient ruins of In-Sa-Ra on Kusaie Island; the Nahnmwarki's investiture platform on Ponape Island; the quarries at Takaiu and Uh, source of Nan Madol's columnar basalt. *Kiti Mangrove Park* would protect portions of

the extensive mangrove swamps near Wene and Rohn Kiti, and would include the tropical forest transition zone on higher land. The transitional forest shelters many varieties of magnificent trees, some of them very large individuals that escaped logging during the Japanese administration. In the tropics, mangrove swamps protect unstable shorelines from typhoon waves, provide important breeding grounds, and are a biochemical buffer zone protecting the clarity and health of lagoons and off-shore barrier reefs. The Kiti swamp is one of the finest in Micronesia, and should be protected. High wooden walks, in selected places, would serve as self-guiding trails into the swamp jungle.

Elabaob Oceanic Park

South of Koror Island, administrative center of Palau, lie hundreds of limestone islets. Called the Rock Islands by Americans, and *Elabaob* by Palauans, the islets are up-raised fossil reefs of a configuration that, though not unique to the Palauan archipelago—it occurs also in Aldabra, Guam, and the Philippines—does in Palau reach its apogee. Nowhere do similar islands exist in such numbers and variety. At waterline the islands are oddly undercut. Tiny chitons with teeth of magnetite and several marine microorganisms have eaten away the limestone between tidelines, circumcising each island, setting each islet on a pedestal. Protected from high seas by the barrier reef to the west, the islands densely occupy 200 square miles of lagoon. They are a multitude of puffy hummocks, thickly forested with endemic dort trees of a hardness approaching steel, and numerous other tropical species.

The islands are habitat for estuarine crocodiles, shell-fish, bait fish, turtles, and sea birds. Their jungles are refuge for several endangered endemic species, among them the Micronesian megapode and the Palau Scops owl —both estimated in 1968 to be under 60 pairs—and the crimson-crowned fruit dove and Nicobar pigeon. Adjacent waters are habitat for the dugong, a nearly extinct sea mammal. Nowhere in the world, in the opinion of Robert Owen, Chief Conservationist for the Trust Territory, is there a meeting of marine and terrestrial environments of comparable scientific significance. There are few places where land and sea meet more beautifully.

The interior valleys of certain of the larger islands have village ruins from Palau's prehistory—mounds and middens uncharted and undisturbed. On the evidence of the ruins, there were once many more people in the Elabaob Islands than there are presently. The coral limestone sup-

ports a poor and scanty soil, and agriculture isn't easy. One of the islands has a single family dwelling on it, and several others are visited only by weekend picnickers from Koror. There is presently no conflicting land use that would interfere with a large park. Perhaps this was true in the old days too, for before the 1543 arrival of Ruiz Lopez de Villalobos, "discoverer" of Palau, several of the islands were wildlife reserves, designated as such by the chiefs, each island protecting a different wild species. A twentieth century park in the Elabaob Islands would be a return to old sensibilities.

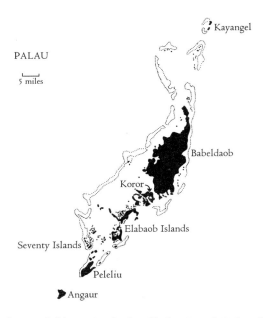

The Park would best include all the Rock Islands south and east of Koror. There is talk in Palau of establishing a park with more modest boundaries, but boundaries that fail to include the entire Elabaob labyrinth will be a mistake, regretted later. An ambitious park would assure that skin diving, boating, and fishing—the age-old uses of these waters—will remain the future uses.

Peleliu Oceanic Park

The bloodiest battle in the Pacific, for the land area gained, occurred on Peleliu Island of the Palau group. It was a battle that, in the opinion of Admiral "Bull" Halsey, was unnecessary. Three days before the invasion of Peleliu, planes from Halsey's Third Fleet swept the central Philippines so successfully that there were no more targets available. Halsey radioed the Pacific Command headquarters that the planned invasion of Peleliu was no longer vital. Possession of the Western Carolines was not essential to an American seizure of the Philippines, he said, and only Ulithi Atoll needed to be taken as a fleet anchorage. Headquarters disagreed.

On September 15, 1944, the American attack force arrived off Peleliu in perfect weather. The Japanese were asleep. They had not detected the U.S. fleet of battleships, carriers, and supporting ships. Advance carrier strike forces surprised 127 enemy fighters and bombers parked on Peleliu's airstrip, destroying them on the ground. With control of the air, an eventual American victory was never in doubt.

But the Japanese had been busy. The commanding officer of Japanese forces in the Marianas, lost to the Americans two months before, had arrived in Koror by submarine to assume command of Palau. Full of his recent experience of American amphibious assaults, he expedited the construction of interconnecting tunnels and caves on Peleliu, decided against the wasteful "banzai" charges that had failed on Saipan, and ordered his troops to stay underground during the heavy pre-assault bombardment by American ships and planes. Through three days, six thousand rounds of high explosive naval ordinance, and tons of bombs, the Japanese troops stayed below ground. When American marines disembarked from landing craft outside the reef, they did not receive a single hostile shot. They transferred to "amtracks" and "ducks," and after a final rocket barrage by the LST's they reached shore. The first marines to step from the armored shelter of their tracked vehicles met a withering fire from Japanese positions in defilade.

The battle lasted for twenty-eight days. The center of Japanese strength was Umurbrogol Mountain, quickly renamed "Bloody Nose Ridge," by the G.I.'s. After the three days of preparatory bombardment, the ridge was a Hellish landscape of broken trees and bare, dark pinnacles of limestone and phosphate rock. The battle fought there was nightmarish and insane. At times in the course of the fighting the Americans held the top of the ridge, and the Japanese the caves in the cliffs below. American planes flew missions from the Japanese-built Peleliu airfield before its approaches were fully secured. The pilots made what must have been the shortest bombing runs in history, dropping their bombs on enemy positions before their wheels were fully retracted. Bloody Nose Ridge began 300 yards north of the runway.

As Peleliu was secured, unknown hundreds of Japanese were buried alive inside their vast network of tunnels. The entrances were sealed one by one, and Peleliu became its defenders' tomb. Most remain entombed today. Many of the entrances not obscured by jungle are still too dangerous to enter—booby-trapped with explosives. Abandoned tanks rust in the forest, and coastal guns rust on the hillsides. Coral-surfaced roads built during the U.S. occupa-

tion crisscross the island, running toward destinations that no longer exist. They are traveled only by land crabs, and by public work crews that for some reason keep them clear of vegetation. At a high point of Bloody Nose Ridge stands a slender stone monument, with an inscription in steel, itself now corroded and scarcely legible. "Lest we forget," reads the monument. Peleliu Oceanic Park would convey the same message.

In Palau there are numerous sites of importance to the history of the archipelago, and deserving of protection: *Arakabesang Terraces* District Historical Site—shaped-earth terraces high on the side of the island. No explanation of their origin exists in Palauan folklore or oral history. They may have been constructed for agricultural purposes. *Ongelunge Rock Paintings* site—limestone cliffs painted in ocher, mostly abstract, except for one recognizable canoe. *Oimad el Marach Rock Paintings*—among which is a deerlike animal in red ochre, a mystery in islands with no large mammals. *Babeldaob Quarry*, in Omisch Cave on Koror, where the Yapese mined the great stone disks they used for money. Several unfinished pieces, six to eight feet in diameter, remain. And *Badrilau Megaliths*, protecting the Badrilau megaliths.

Helen Reef is an isolated island in the extreme southwest corner of the Palau District, and thus of Micronesia. The island is extraordinarily abundant with reef fish, turtles, giant clams, and birdlife (terns, boobies, and frigate birds). It is uninhabited and pristine, free of rats, flies, and mosquitoes, though subject to poaching by crews of Okinawan tuna boats and other vessels. Helen Reef should become *Helen Reef Wildlife Preserve*, with visitation limited to scientists with a reason.

In 1956 the Palau Legislature declared that all land, water, reef, and underwater areas of the island group known as Ngerukewid (also called the Seventy Islands) would be "retained in its present primitive condition, where the natural plant and animal life shall be permitted to develop undisturbed." Entry to the Seventy Islands was restricted. This preserve would remain a protected sanctuary within Elabaob Oceanic Park.

Arno Atoll Oceanic Park

Arno is a classic atoll, stuff for a South Sea fiction writer's dreams. Miles of curved, white-sand beach, fringed by coconut palms, encircle a many-hued lagoon. The turquoise of the shallow waters is reflected in the cumulus clouds above—a beacon for returning canoes a hundred miles distant. Arno's 133 islands are scattered around a lagoon of 130 square miles, yet they themselves add up to only five square miles of earth. No land in Arno stands higher than six feet above the sea. Some of the islets are simple sand spits, curving briefly above the water. Others support shrubs, beach vine, and perhaps a coconut palm or two. The larger islands are forested with pandanus, banana, some papaya and lime trees, arrowroot in great quantities, breadfruit, coconuts, and small plantings of sweet potatoes.

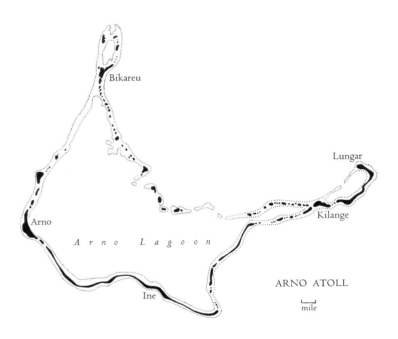

Virtually every species of plant on Arno has a use in medicine, home-construction, canoe-building, weaving, dyeing, or as food. Most plant species are introduced, either long ago by Micronesian settlers or in the past hundred years of control by foreign powers. Only 44 plant species are native, a small number compared to the floras of the high islands of Micronesia, but large compared to other low atolls, farther from the Malaysian and Melanesian sources of seeds.

Arno is habitat for 175 or more species of fish and invertebrates. The only resident land birds are heron and pigeon, but Pacific terns, various shore birds, and the migratory golden plover are sometimes seen island-hopping. Arno is full of termites—all dead wood is riddled by them. The Marshallese alternative to pesticides is to cut wood green, soak it for several weeks, weighted down with stones, in the lagoon's salt water, then build termite-proof houses with it. The earthworms of Arno are very active, twisting and turning violently when disturbed, jumping several inches into the air. A foraging bird has great difficulty taking flight with an Arno worm alive in its beak, and Arno children bet on the worm.

The human population is about 800, probably the maximum number allowable if Arno's environmental and cultural integrity is to be maintained. There are no roads or cars on Arno. The people live the Marshallese village life of a hundred years ago. Arno is still famous for its love school, where mothers sent their daughters to learn the arts of love. (Arno residents, weary now of the curiosity of outsiders, deny that the school still exists, and perhaps it doesn't.) The school's instructors were older women, and men were excluded. Graduates of the school are admired throughout the Marshalls, and are referred to proudly by their husbands as "Arno girls." Arno has its own way of preparing breadfruit, too, in addition to all the conventional methods. Thirty or forty whole, unpeeled breadfruit are placed in a copra bag and soaked in the lagoon. After a month the fruit is peeled, its mushy meat mixed with spices, kneaded, and cooked over an open fire. Poured into a pit lined with breadfruit and banana leaves, then covered and weighted down with rocks, the breadfruit is allowed to ferment for three months. The *piro,* as the mixture is called, is then shaped into fist-sized balls and served with roast pig. It smells terrible to a visitor, but no feast is really a feast without piro.

Majuro, the district center, ten miles away, is different. Majuro has a "Navy culture," in which the traditional characteristics of Marshallese life are no longer recognizable. Hundreds work for the government. Unskilled labor on public works projects is the kind of work to get, if you can. Copra-harvesting and fishing is work to avoid. It is easy to avoid building thatch houses now, or growing yams and fishing in traditional ways, for no one remembers how. Building canoes is unnecessary—you can buy a Boston Whaler, with molded fiberglass hull and Mercury outboard, straight from the catalog. Or a Datsun taxi. That the materials are available locally to build canoes, but not taxis, and that enough taxis, for long enough, will make the people dependent on sources in distant mainlands, has not slowed their eagerness for such things.

In Micronesia, native navigational systems are localized. The sailor's problem in the Marshalls is different from his problem in the Carolines, where navigators learn to hold their course in relation to uninterrupted swells whose origin they learn to identify. There are no such swells in the Marshalls. Marshallese navigators instead have to decipher the wave-interference patterns set up by the many atolls of Marshallese waters. The descendants of men who could read in the waves the relative position of the surrounding unseen atolls that made their universe, now navigate, in Datsuns and Toyotas, Majuro's few miles of road.

Majuro is made up of three former islands: Djarrit, Uliga, and Dalap, now combined by Navy bulldozers, by means of causeways of crushed coral, into a single, long, narrow island scarcely a thousand feet wide for most of its length. The memory of the individual islands lives still in their initials, stenciled on Majuro's tiny police cars: "DUD," the aptness of which is lost on Marshallese-speaking people.

Following a recent New Zealand Medical study of Pacific peoples—part of which was a survey of 2500 residents of Ponape Island—Dr. Ian Prior, the research director, reported that Pacific natives are "now commencing to suffer for the first time in their history from the same degenerative diseases that are the primary causes of death among white men . . . it does not seem too much to say our evidence now shows that the farther the Pacific natives move from the quiet, carefree life of their ancestors, the closer they come to gout, diabetes, arteriosclerosis, obesity, and hypertension." The notion that the life of the ancestors was carefree is romantic perhaps, but Dr. Prior's studies confirm what many of us have secretly suspected—that life in a thatched hut is best after all. Speed does kill, it seems. In an outrigger canoe you get there slower, but live longer. The material benefits of civilization are more expensive than current accounting practices indicate. Cost-benefit analyses should include a column on death.

Arno Atoll Oceanic Park would be dedicated to life, and to the sensible pace at which it is presently lived on the atoll's islands. (Establishment of a park would depend, of course, on the desire of Arno's people to have one.)

Elsewhere in the Marshalls, *Majuro Beach Park* would preserve the beaches on either side of the point of land beyond Laura Village, and the island's ultimate sand bar. The area includes operating fish traps, magnificent ocean and lagoon swimming, and a vast shallow-water coral reef. *Bikini Historical Park* would include the remains of Boknejen Island (Baker), and Bokbata (Able), both reduced to sandbars by the first hydrogen bomb. The Park would be a monument to man's ingenuity. Designated as historical sites would be the cemetery for Marshallese chiefs on Buoj Island, Ailinlaplap Atoll; the de Brum family home on Likiep Island of Likiep Atoll—a well maintained example of turn-of-the-century plantation-home architecture; and the monument erected by the Japanese in Majuro to commemorate the 1918 typhoon and the Emperor's relief measures.

Marpi Oceanic Park

Marpi Oceanic Park on the island of Saipan, in the Marianas, would be dedicated both to history and to scenery. The park would include the abandoned Northwest Field airbase, now overgrown with tangentangen except for the runways; and the Banzai and Suicide cliffs, from which mass suicides by Japanese Imperial troops followed the failure of their last stand against American forces. On the proposed park's western boundary is the site of the last Japanese command post, a cavern at the base of Marpi Cliff, from which Japanese generals directed their last desperate counterattacks. In spite of its dark history, Marpi Park will not be grim. Today Suicide Cliff carries its name lightly—from its top there are panoramic and sunny views of Saipan's rocky coastline. On the northeast shore is the Blue Grotto, a sunken limestone cave into which the ocean ebbs and flows through subterranean passages. The Grotto is swimmable to the daring, and a luminescent, backlit blue glow to the sightseer. The park would protect Wing Beach on the west, and the high cliffs and wooded shore to the east, as well as Bird Island off the eastern shore.

To a non-Micronesian reader, the proposed park system may seem at this point unnecessarily martial, but such has been Micronesia's history. The battle for the Marianas was fierce, and has made for other war-memorial parks. *Blue Beach District Park* would commemorate the spot where U.S. troops first landed, code-named "Blue Beach," and would double as a recreational park. It would include the lagoon out to the barrier reef, the Sherman tank in the lagoon, the entire beach and all land between beach and shore road, and the road-junction memorials to U.S. troops. *Tinian District Park* would mark an event in the history of warfare that is more than just epochal. On August 6 and 9, 1945, the Hiroshima and Nagasaki A-bombs were loaded into B-29 superfortresses on Tinian's North Field. The two open pits from which the bombs were loaded now each grows a coconut palm—symbolic, we can only hope. *Garapan Municipal Park* on Saipan would identify and protect the ruins of a portion of the Japanese town of Garapan, including the old church tower, the Japanese jail where Amelia Erhart was reportedly held, the hospital ruins, and the remains of the Japanese gardens—the flowering trees of which, with some new planting and landscaping, could become one of the most beautiful "city" parks in Micronesia.

Tinian Municipal Park would reserve the popular white-sand beach near San Jose village for its highest use; recreation. *House of Taga Historical Site* would protect the ancient Chamorro village on Tinian said to be the home of Chief Taga, the Paul Bunyan of the Marianas. *Rota Island Wildlife Preserve* would give additional, park-system protection to Taipingot Peninsula, where wild deer and birds now abound through the conservation regulations of Rota municipality. *Pagan Island District Park* would protect the volcano of Pagan, the most active volcano in the Marianas, with its fuming mountain cone and hot springs.

Truk Lagoon Oceanic Park

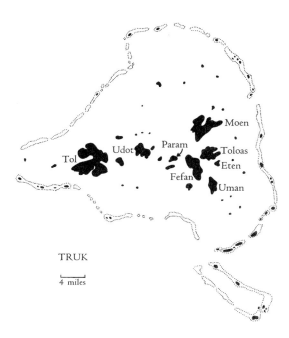

TRUK

4 miles

In the Truk District the major park would be, for the most part, underwater. *Truk Lagoon Oceanic Park* would encompass the old Japanese fleet anchorages between the islands of Moen, Toloas, Fefan, and Tol, beneath the waters of which lie an estimated forty sunken warships and merchantmen. Twenty of the wrecks are well known and accessible to scuba divers, who consider these waters to be among the most exciting in the world. The park would set aside Toloas Island as a war memorial, preserving the island's Japanese underground power-generation tunnels, water-purification plant, bank, reefer, soap factory, jail, radio station, pill boxes, piers, wharfs, and petroleum tanks. A complementary *Truk Lagoon District Park* would reserve for use by the people numerous small, uninhabited islets on the barrier reef and inside the lagoon, all eminently suited for picnic areas, campsites, and fishing spots. *Tol Island District Park* would preserve in its na-

tural state the 1200-foot mountain of Tol, highest in the Truk Lagoon, and the surrounding tropical rain forest.

In the Yap District, Balebat Village on Yap Island, a major storage place for Yapese stone money, would become a historical site, as would the island where "His Majesty" O'Keefe built, from the proceeds of his stone-money trade, his mansion. The ruins of the mansion, among which lie tiles O'Keefe imported from China, are buried now in jungle.

* * *

Outside of the parks listed here, as we have said, there is a vast de facto wilderness. The threats to this wilderness are not so pressing as the threats to the larger, settled islands on which technology has established its beach-heads. The immediate dangers to the wilderness are of the widespread, global variety—marine pollution by pesticides, oil slicks, and other human effluvia—that no system of parks can defend against. But ever since Charles Darwin and his observations in the Galapagos, the great value of undisturbed islands as scientific laboratories has been manifest. A select series of uninhabited islands in the Micronesian wilderness should be set aside as scientific preserves, available for research by scientists of all nations. Visits by casual visitors would be forbidden by act of the Micronesian Congress. In the Marianas, the islands of Maug, Farrallon de Medinilla, Guguan, and Uracas (Farallon de Pajaros) would become preserves; in the Marshalls, Pokak (Taongi) Atoll and Bikar Atoll; and in the Eastern Carolines, East Fayu. Helen Reef and the Seventy Islands of Palau, previously mentioned, would be part of this system. A portion of the Marianas Trench south of Guam—the deepest waters of Earth—would become an international undersea preserve.

This, then, is the proposal. We hope the Micronesian people will see merit in it.

Guam National Seashore

In the controversy over a proposed National Seashore on the southwest coast of Guam, there is a lesson for all Micronesia. Guam is U.S. territory, and there, unlike the U.S. *Trust* Territory—the 2,202 other islands of Micronesia—the people vote in national elections and elect their own governor. Guam's people presumably have some small political power. Their brothers in the Trust Territory have none. Therefore, the powerlessness of Guam's people, in the face of U.S. Navy designs on their Seashore, should serve as a warning, in spades, to other islanders.

The strength of the military in the Pacific, and the weakness of democratic processes there, has profound implications for a Micronesian park system such as we have described, as well as for freedom.

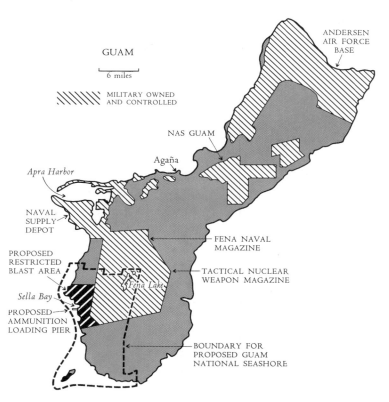

GUAM

6 miles

MILITARY OWNED
AND CONTROLLED

NAS GUAM

Agaña

Apra Harbor

NAVAL
SUPPLY
DEPOT

PROPOSED
RESTRICTED
BLAST AREA

Sella Bay

PROPOSED
AMMUNITION
LOADING PIER

ANDERSEN
AIR FORCE
BASE

FENA NAVAL
MAGAZINE

Fena Lake

TACTICAL NUCLEAR
WEAPON MAGAZINE

BOUNDARY FOR
PROPOSED GUAM
NATIONAL SEASHORE

The southwest coast of Guam is the last wild area of any size on a heavily populated western Pacific island. About the size of Molokai in Hawaii, Guam has a population of 90,000 and a birth rate as high as any in the world. The military owns or controls more than one-third of the island, and urban developments and sprawling residential communities occupy most of the rest. Chance has spared the southwest coast from the pressures of such human numbers and human uses. There is great natural beauty along the south shore and in the grassy hills above. The fringing reef provides shelter from storms, and thus the opportunity to develop a wide range of sea-oriented recreational activities. The area is important to science. The University of Guam has proposed an Underwater Conservation Area there, with boundaries extending from the shore to a depth of 400 feet. Much of the area would be designated "multi-use," with portions set aside as restricted marine sanctuaries. University scientists note that the area includes the richest coral communities on the island as yet undisturbed by man or the crown-of-thorns starfish. The area is full of historical interest. Latte stones and other ruins of Chamorro civilization abound. The four centuries of European presence in Guam have left their mark. Ferdinand Magellan, whose ship first circumnavigated the globe, anchored in Cetti Bay. Sir Francis Drake paused here. Treasure galleons bound from Acapulco to Manila stopped at Umatac Bay to reprovision, guided by signal fires atop Mount Lamlam, the highest point on Guam. Today Umatac Village, with its church ruins and the three forts guarding the Bay, is still a Spanish town.

In 1965, after a two-month field trip, a National Park Service study team recommended that Guam National Seashore be established on the southwest shore. The Territory of Guam Master Plan, 1966, supported the idea. In 1967 a second Park Service team visited, and renewed the proposal. A working draft of their report read, "the Advisory Board on National Parks, Historic Sites, Buildings and Monuments considered the national seashore proposal during their April 17-19, 1967 meeting . . . The Board . . . recommends that the Secretary of the Interior seek administrative approval of this proposal and that the proposed legislation be transmitted to the Congress to accomplish this worthwhile objective."

For four years the Department of Interior did nothing to implement these recommendations. The study-team report was not released, even when it was requested by resolution of the Guam Legislature. On Guam the rumor was that the Guam Seashore conflicted with Navy plans for expansion of their ammunition facilities, and that Navy had asked Interior to defer approval of the park. Interior gave no reason for its inaction. Letters to the Secretary from citizens of Guam drew no response. (The 1967 study team had recommended that a War in the Pacific National Historical Park be established to the north of the Seashore—in an area where the Navy had no interests—and just eight months later *that* park was approved.)

At Sella Bay, in the heart of the proposed Seashore, the Navy wanted to construct an ammunition pier to provide increased storage capacity and safer handling facilities on Guam for tactical nuclear munitions from Okinawa. In the preliminary draft of what would prove a tardy and elusive Environmental Impact Statement on the Sella Bay project (not submitted for review until twelve months after Congress authorized funds for land acquisition and engineering), the Navy began its description of the project in a disarming manner. "Construction of the pier at Sella Bay will require minor clearing of existing vegetation in a small area near the beach, earthmoving, grading and stabilizing of access road and land in the support facilities area, dredging and stabilizing of ship berths . . . approximately 15 acres of land in this area will be disturbed during construction." The more frightening dimensions of the pier are buried in the engineering terminology that followed. The project "consists of an ammunition loading/unloading facility including a 350 ft. (wide) x 700 ft.

(long) earth filled pier with associated navigational aids; shoreside support buildings, parking lot and utilities, and a 1½ mile access road . . . Land acquisition of 845 acres of privately owned land and 2875 acres of Government of Guam land within a 10,400 foot radius of the pier as an explosive safety zone. . . ."

All in the middle of the proposed Seashore, Guam's last wild place. The earth-fill would occur in the marine conservation area proposed by the University of Guam.

In the hills above Sella Bay there is a valley called Fena. At the bottom of the valley, beneath rolling hills and tropical vegetation, is Fena Valley Reservoir, two miles long and half a mile wide. The waters of the reservoir are home for two species of bass and other warm-water game fish. The bass are presently in no danger from fishermen, and the beauty of the hills presently goes unseen, for the reservoir and valley are part of Fena Naval Magazine, a restricted military reservation. In its unreleased study-team report, the Park Service recommended that the valley be included in the Seashore. "The Department of Defense holdings in the Fena Valley area should be transferred to the Department of Interior," the report suggested, because, "restricted military use is incompatible with park purposes." (Fena Valley is said to contain some of Guam's better archaeological sites, but it is hard to know for sure, for the Navy would not allow the study team to inspect the area.) It was Fena Magazine that the Navy planned to expand to receive the munitions unloaded at the Sella Bay pier, though the Navy would keep quiet about the expansion, and the people of Guam would not learn of it for some time.

A single-column legal notice appeared in the *Pacific Daily News,* announcing a public hearing on June 1, 1970, to discuss proposed Resolution No. 331, "expressing utter opposition of the people of Guam to the proposed acquisition by the Department of Defense of Sella Bay and its environs for the construction of an ammunition wharf." On the appointed day, a standing-room-only crowd showed up, and made clear their wish that the pier go elsewhere. A majority of witnesses felt that since the military already owned one-third of the island, it should be able to find an adequate site within an existing military reservation on Guam.

Navy Captain R.H.P. Dunn reassured the gathering that, "The Navy has no objection to development of the Sella Bay area for an underwater park. There is no reason why an underwater park could not be developed and used by the public." But if the Navy had no objections to sharing Sella Bay, the audience did. An earth-filled pier the size of four football fields, jutting out over the coral reef, and the ecological consequences of pollution by large ammunition ships, did not to everyone seem compatible with a marine preserve. (Later, when other Navy spokesmen proposed "multi-use recreational facilities for the public in the area that will be required for the wharf and the safety zone surrounding it," Guamanians would wonder exactly what that meant. Races between ammunition ships and water skiers to see who gets to the pier first? Easter Sunday bomb rolling?)

Guam Senator B. J. Bordallo read his opinions into the record. To the Senator it seemed that the Navy was offering "every kind of sugar-coated promise" to gain acquiescence for a project already begun. "Here in our community, Mr. Speaker, it seems that major governmental actions with impact on the community become known only after such actions reach irreversible stages. The case of Sella Bay is a perfect example. I daresay that if it were not for a conflict between the interests of the land speculators and the military, the whole ammunition wharf would have been completed before the people of Guam woke up to the fact."

At the end of the three-hour public meeting, Resolution 331 was adopted.

Resistance to the Navy was slow in building, however. Few American communities are so economically dependent on the military as is Guam's. The people of the island are careful, quite reasonably, about chewing too vigorously on the hand that feeds them. On Guam there is considerable loyalty to the Services, and rightly so. One of the civilian bastions of military strength, on the Sella Bay issue, was the Guam Chamber of Commerce. The Executive Vice President of the Chamber was Retired Admiral Carlton Jones. Before he retired, Jones had been the successor of Admiral Cole, who in 1968 had originally proposed the Sella Bay pier. Admiral Jones, in a statement filed with the Guam Legislature and with the local newspaper and radio, described the Navy's engineering and logistical investigations of Sella Bay in detail, then dismissed any further debate as academic. He reminded the Guam Legislature that the U.S. Congress, "has approved $3,327,000 for this controversial ammunition area at Sella Bay. . . The Chief of Naval Operations has directed that plans be continued for relocating the Ammunition Wharf to Sella Bay. This action, of course, effectively precludes the necessity for any further action such as the subject Resolution." (The Navy had decided; therefore the "utter opposition of the people of Guam," as expressed in Resolution 331, was foolish.)

Members of the Chamber of Commerce were never

polled on the matter. Admiral Jones simply declared it a non-issue. As he said, the Navy was going ahead anyway. Several members promptly resigned, and the controversy grew warmer. (When Robert Wenkam, Pacific Representative of Friends of the Earth (FOE), later asked Admiral Jones if the ammunition pier was really needed, he answered, "If the Navy can't have Sella Bay, the Navy would have to leave Guam. National security demands Sella Bay." It may be so, but such an answer comes very easily to military men.)

In January, 1970, the Guam Environmental Council, (GEC), was organized. The first item on the GEC agenda was Sella Bay. Paul Souder, the first GEC President, wrote to the Commander of Naval Forces in the Marianas, asking to review the Navy's environmental impact report on Sella Bay. Receiving no impact statement there (the Navy had none to give), GEC then wrote letters to President Nixon and to Russell Train, Chairman of the President's Council on Environmental Quality, and asked again. (An environmental impact statement is required by law. Public Law 91-190 reads, in part: "Included in every recommendation or report on proposals for legislation and other major Federal actions significantly affecting the quality of the human environment, shall be a detailed statement by the responsible official. . . .")

In the President's reply to the GEC letter—a reply written by Frank Sanders, Assistant Secretary of the Navy—the GEC was assured of "coordinated planning for the Sella Bay area and the establishment of joint use of the area by the Navy and the National Park Service." The GEC had yet to see the impact statement.

Robert Wenkam, the FOE representative, had been working to advance the Seashore idea since its inception. In 1966, under contract to the Guam government, he had made a photographic inventory of Guam's scenic resources for use in the tourist promotion program then just underway. The Director of the Guam Tourist Commission had encouraged the photographer to push for the park, as had Manuel Guerrero, then Governor of Guam. Wenkam was anxious now to discover if an impact statement existed.

Representative Patsy Mink of Hawaii, acting on a request by FOE, joined in the quest by writing to the Department of the Interior and asking for the impact statement. Her letter was forwarded to Frank Sanders, Assistant Navy Secretary, who in April 1971 answered that, "The Navy will prepare an environmental impact statement on this project if it is included in the President's Fiscal Year 1973 Budget." It was a strange answer. Congressional hearings had been held on the Sella Bay pierhead more than a year before (March 13, 1970), and five months

before, in November 1970, $3,287,000 had been approved for classified expansion of Fena Magazine and land acquisition at Sella Bay. Such tardiness in filing would be, and was, in violation of federal law. Later, when FOE inquired at the Honolulu District Office of the Corps of Engineers, it discovered that the Navy, in proceeding with land acquisition surveys for the pierhead, had not bothered, either, to request the required Corps permit for "construction in navigable waters."

(In 1972, the Fena Magazine expansion was completed, the nuclear-weapons igloos all constructed, yet no impact statement was ever filed for the magazine.)

FOE was able to study portions of the then-unfiled environmental impact statement for the pier construction. It seems to be based, for the most part, on information gathered by the Urban Grad-Wall firm, which investigated pier alternatives in 1968 under Navy Contract NBY 87267. The statement refers to Sella Bay as "very rugged, desolate." According to the statement, an ammunition transport would be an "improvement," for "the proposed construction will provide access." (In the Park Service report, not released to the public until 1972, but then in the Navy's possession, the study team argued against any road to Sella Bay, in order to preserve the natural values. Instead, they suggested, "trails from Facpi Point will lead to the shore and tide pools.") For advocates of the Seashore, the Navy's access principle was too much like Vietnam's: the military wanted to destroy the village in order to save it. But the Navy was pleased with the statement. Rear Admiral Spencer Smith, writing in *Pac-Facts,* said, "Our first impact statement was prepared recently for the proposed ammunition wharf at Sella Bay, Guam. I am proud to report that it has been well received in Washington, and it may well be used as a prototype for future Navy environmental impact statements."

On Guam, Sella Bay was becoming a controversy of major proportions. A "Save Sella Bay" petition was circulated by the GEC, asking the Department of Interior to establish a Guam National Park on the southwest shore.

On February 24, 1971, the Guam Legislature adopted Resolution No.158. The Resolution states that, "one of the more vital issues affecting the people of Guam is the proposed acquisition by the Federal Government of Sella Bay and the area surrounding it for use by the Navy as an ammunition wharf, the land in question being an unspoiled and unexploited part of Guam bordering on the Pacific Ocean that is not only beautiful and of great recreational potential but is also a unique example in the American commonwealth of a Pacific reef environment that should be studied and preserved for future generations.

"The Legislature is advised that the proposed acquisition will include 4,400 acres, almost 3 per cent of the whole land area of Guam, and yet of those 4,400 acres only 10 acres are actually needed for the dock site, the remaining land only being allegedly necessary because of the potential damage which would be caused by a Port Chicago type of explosion at the wharf, the Navy promising that the remaining land will be open to the public and that the historic artifacts and the unique coral ecology will supposedly be preserved, and while no one wishes to question the good faith of the members of the local Navy command who are currently making these assurances, it is ineluctable that once the United States acquires the fee title to the 4,400 acres no resident of Guam nor agency of the territorial government will be in a position to enforce these commitments. . . .

"The Legislature has in the past adopted a series of resolutions asking reconsideration by the Department of Defense on this proposed taking and otherwise presenting the opposition of the people of Guam thereto, but no response has ever been afforded to these anguished pleas. . . .

"Resolved, that the Eleventh Guam Legislature does hereby go on record in firm support of the Nixon Doctrine first enunciated in Guam by our President in June of 1969, which doctrine clearly and unequivocably spells out the commitment by the United States of America to change its defense posture in the Pacific from one of actively and aggressively defending this area from communism to one of assisting the people of Asia to defend themselves, the whole profile of America in the Pacific being lowered . . . respectively pointing out that its opposition to the Sella Bay acquisition is in furtherance and support of the Nixon Doctrine, the people of Guam wondering how the defenders of this doctrine can ever hope to defend the acquisition of another 3 per cent of Guam over the unanimous opposition of its people. . . .

"Resolved, that, congruent to the Nixon Doctrine, the Eleventh Guam Legislature does hereby on behalf of the people of Guam express the fervent desire of all the inhabitants of this territory for a new image for Guam—an image not of a large military base, armed to the teeth, and aggressively poised to bomb Vietnam or threaten Red China, but of a peaceful South Pacific tourist site, with friendly people and open beaches. . . ."

It was a strong Resolution, full of doubts about the military, yet when the legislators wrote it they had not read the Park Service recommendations for the Seashore, nor were they aware of the Navy's plans to expand Fena Magazine into the area proposed for the Seashore. At a press conference arranged by the Guam Press Club, Friends of the Earth revealed these things. The newsmen learned that the Department of Interior had given the Navy the study-team report, but had not seem fit to share it with the people of Guam or their Legislature. The Navy had misrepresented the case for Sella Bay. For four days running it was a front page story. The Guam Legislature was furious.

The Guam Legislature passed a new resolution, asking that FOE, a citizen environmental organization, help stop construction of the Sella Bay pier, and help establish a Guam National Seashore.

FOE's representative, Wenkam, met with Navy officials and the Environmental Protection Agency (EPA) in Washington, and requested that an impact statement be filed as required by law, and that the National Park Service release its Guam Seashore report. The EPA wrote the Navy to protest construction of nuclear weapon storage igloos within the area proposed for a park. The reply was unsatisfactory and the EPA wrote again, asking why an impact statement had not been filed before construction, as required by law. The Navy answered by memo that the Secretary would reply by telephone. He did so, stating that because storage of tactical nuclear weapons on Guam was necessary for national security, the Navy did not find it necessary to file. They would file an impact statement on the pier, however. (The Navy decided to obey the law half way. The Federal Government, the EPA at least, was as powerless in the face of this decision as the people of Guam, apparently.)

Shortly afterward, EPA officials telephoned FOE, suggesting that the organization drop its opposition to the pier, in return for which the Navy would fully support the establishment of the Guam Seashore, with adequate appropriations and public access to bomb blast areas. FOE argued, as it argues still, that such a compromise would create a very unusual recreation area, including as it did nuclear storage magazines and ammunition loading pier in the center of the park.

Within a month a bill to establish a Guam National Seashore was introduced in Congress. There the matter stands today. The battle for an uncompromised, pierless park continues, but against one of the most formidably powerful institutions in history. The lesson for Micronesia is clear. In the Trust Territory of the Pacific Islands, under the terms of the U.N. mandate, the U.S. may build military bases wherever it pleases. If the power of the military is not quite absolute in Guam, it is in the other islands of Micronesia. The U.S. public can require a change.

R.W. and K.B.

September, 1972

Voyages without islands to touch upon would be epics of monotony. This was the attitude of the seventeenth century adventurers, and so it was later to prove with the time travelers in the new science of geology. We may equally expect to encounter similar views in the future annals of the astronauts. Whether for diversion of thought or for the easing of the physical body, men demand mental periods, points of reference, islands fixed in the turbulence of giant waters or, if eluding the compass, still haunting the mind. . . .

—LOREN EISELEY

…islands fixed in the turbulence

Six months at sea! Yes, reader, as I live, six months out of sight of land; cruising after the sperm-whale beneath the scorching sun of the Line, and tossed on the billows of the wide-rolling Pacific—the sky above, the sea around, and nothing else!

—HERMAN MELVILLE, *Typee*

Now would I give a thousand furlongs of sea for an acre of barren ground—long heath, brown furze, anything. The wills above be done! but I would fain die a dry death.

—SHAKESPEARE, *The Tempest*

. . . as the rage of the wind was still great, though rather less than at first, we could not so much as hope to have the ship hold many minutes without breaking in pieces, unless the winds, by a kind of miracle, should turn immediately about. In a word, we sat looking one upon another, and expecting death every moment, and every man acting accordingly as preparing for another world.

—DANIEL DEFOE, *Robinson Crusoe*

Thunderhead, Arno Channel, Marshall Islands

Borne toward the rock,
He clutched it instantly with both his hands,
And panting clung till that huge wave rolled by,
And so escaped its fury. Back it came,
And smote him once again, and flung him far
Seaward. As to the claws of Polypus,
Plucked from its bed, the pebbles thickly cling,
So flakes of skin, from off his powerful hands,
Were left upon the rock. The mighty surge
O'erwhelmed him; he had perished ere his time,—
Hapless Ulysses!—but the blue-eyed maid,
Pallas, informed his mind with forecast. Straight
Emerging from the wave that shoreward rolled,
He swam along the coast and eyed it well,
In hope of sloping beach or sheltered creek.
But when, in swimming, he had reached the mouth
Of a soft-flowing river, here appeared
The spot he wished for, smooth, without a rock,
And here was shelter from the wind. He felt
The current's flow, and thus devoutly prayed:—

    "Hear me, O sovereign power, whoe'ver thou art!
To thee, the long-desired, I come. I seek
Escape from Neptune's threatenings on the sea.
The deathless gods respect the prayer of him
Who looks to them for help, a fugitive,
As I am now, when to thy stream I come,
And to thy knees, from many a hardship past.
O thou that here art ruler, I declare
Myself thy suppliant; be thou merciful."

    He spoke; the river stayed his current, checked
The billows, smoothed them to a calm, and gave
The swimmer a safe landing at his mouth.
Then dropped his knees and sinewy arms at once,
Unstrung, for faint with struggling was his heart.

—HOMER, The Odyssey

I was now landed and safe on shore, and began to look up and thank God that my life was saved in a case wherein there was some minutes before scarce any room for hope. I believe it is impossible to express to the life what the ecstasies and transports of the soul are, when it is so saved, as I may say, out of the very grave. I walked about on the shore, lifting up my hands, and my whole being, as I may say, wrapt up in the contemplation of my deliverance, making a thousand gestures and motions which I cannot describe, reflecting upon all my comrades that were drowned, and that there should not be one soul saved but myself; for, as for them, I never saw them afterwards, or any sign of them, except three of their hats, one cap, and two shoes that were not fellows.

—ROBINSON CRUSOE

Eroded limestone, Laura beach, Marshalls

At 4 a Clock, to our great Joy, we saw the Island Guam, at
about 8 leagues distance.

It was well for Captain Swan that we got sight of it before our
Provision was spent, of which we had but enough for 3 days more;
for, as I was afterwards informed, the Men had contrived, first to kill
Captain Swan and eat him when the Victuals was gone, and after him all
of us who were accessary in promoting the undertaking this Voyage. This
made Captain Swan say to me after our arrival at Guam, Ah! Dampier,
you would have made them but a poor Meal; for I was as lean as the
Captain was lusty and fleshy.

—William Dampier

Not alone did the reading of voyages become popular, but the rough-hewn voyagers themselves began to respond to the demand for greater accuracy and more dispassionate accounts of peoples and places visited. Dampier as an individual almost disappears from his journal, yet his simple and unaffected narration is known to have influenced the style of such literary professionals as Daniel Defoe and Jonathan Swift. The *New Voyage* [Dampier's journal] formed the model for more than one fictional or satiric journey, but its importance extended beyond this: it revealed that the voyagers themseves were growing conscious of a newly forming scientific tradition. They were writing increasingly for a sophisticated public that wanted truth rather than fantasy.

—LOREN EISELEY

The Soil of the Island [Guam] is reddish, dry and indifferent fruitful. The Fruits are chiefly Rice, Pine-Apples, Water-melons, Musk-melons, Oranges and Limes, Coco-nuts, and a sort of Fruit called by us Bread-fruit.

The Coco-nut Trees grow by the Sea, on the Western side in great Groves, 3 or 4 Miles in length, and a Mile or two broad. This Tree is in shape like the Cabbage-tree, and at a distance they are not to be known each from other, only the Coco-nut Tree is fuller of Branches; but the Cabbage-tree generally is much higher, tho' the Coco-nut Trees in some places are very high.

The Nut or Fruit grows at the head of the Tree, among the Branches and in Clusters, 10 or 12 in a Cluster.

. . .

Coconut palms, Arno Beach, Marshalls

The Nut is generally bigger than a Man's Head. The outer Rind is near two Inches thick; before you come to the Shell; the Shell it self is black, thick, and very hard. The Kernel in some Nuts is near an Inch thick, sticking to the inside of the Shell clear round, leaving a hollow in the middle of it, which contains about a Pint, more or less, according to the bigness of the Nut, for some are much bigger than others.

This Cavity is full of sweet, delicate, wholesom and refreshing Water. While the Nut is growing, all the inside is full of this Water, without any Kernel at all; but as the Nut grows towards its Maturity, the Kernel begins to gather and settle round on the inside of the Shell, and is soft like Cream; and as the Nut ripens, it increaseth in substance and becomes hard. The ripe Kernel is sweet enough, but very hard to digest, therefore seldom eaten, unless by Strangers, who know not the effects of it; but while it is young and soft like Pap, some Men will eat it, scraping it out with a Spoon, after they have drunk the Water that was within it. I like the Water best when the Nut is almost ripe, for it is then sweetest and briskest.

When these Nuts are ripe and gathered, the outside Rind becomes of a brown rusty colour; so that one would think that they were dead and dry; yet they will sprout out like Onions, after they have been hanging in the Sun 3 or 4 Months, or thrown about in a House or Ship, and if planted afterward in the Earth, they will grow up to a Tree.

. . .

Seed coconuts, Toloas Island, Truk

Beside the Liquor or Water in the Fruit, there is also a sort of Wine
drawn from the Tree called Toddy, which looks like Whey. It is sweet and
very pleasant, but it is to be drunk within 24 hours after it is drawn, for
afterwards it grows sowre. . . .

The Kernel is much used in making Broath. When the Nut is dry, they
take off the Husk, and giving two good Blows on the middle of the Nut,
it breaks in two equal parts, letting the Water fall on the Ground;
then with a small Iron Rasp made for the purpose, the Kernel or Nut is
rasped out clean, which being put into a little fresh Water, makes it
become white as Milk. In this milky Water they boil a Fowl, or any other
sort of Flesh, and it makes very savory Broath.

But the greatest use of the Kernel is to make Oyl, both for burning and
for frying. The way to make the Oyl is to grate or rasp the Kernel, and steep
it in fresh Water, then boil it, and scum off the Oyl at top as it rises: But
the Nuts that make the Oyl ought to be a long time gathered, so as that the
Kernel may be turning soft and oily.

The Shell of this Nut is used in the East-Indies for Cups, Dishes, Ladles,
Spoons, and in a manner for all eating and drinking Vessels. The Husk of
the Shell is of great use to make Cables; for the dry Husk is full of small
Strings and Threads, which being beaten, become soft, and the other
Substance which was mixt among it falls away like Saw-dust, leaving only
the Strings. These are afterwards spun into long Yarns, and twisted up into
Balls for Convenience: and many of these Rope-Yarns joined together
make good Cables. . . .

I have been the longer on this subject, to give the Reader a particular
Account and the use and profit of a Vegetable, which is possibly of all
others the most generally serviceable to the conveniences, as well as the
necessities of humane Life.

. . .

The Natives are very ingenious beyond any People, in making Boats, or Proes, as they are called in the East-Indies, and therein they take great delight. These are built sharp at both ends; the bottom is of one piece, made like the bottom of a little Canoa, very neatly dug, and left of a good substance. This bottom part is instead of a Keel. It is about 26 or 28 foot long; the under part of this Keel is made round, but inclining to a wedge, and smooth; and the upper part is almost flat, having a very gentle hollow, and is about a foot broad: From hence both sides of the Boat are carried up to about 5 foot high with narrow Plank, not above 4 or 5 inches broad, and each end of the Boat turns up round, very prettily. But what is very singular, one side of the Boat is made perpendicular, like a Wall, while the other side is rounding, made as other Vessels are with a pretty full belly.

. . .

Along the Belly-side of the Boat, parallel with it, at about 6 or 7 foot distance, lies another small Boat, or Canoa, being a Log of very light Wood, almost as long as the great Boat, but not so wide, being not above a foot and an half wide at the upper part, and very sharp like a Wedge at each end. And there are two Bamboes of about 8 or 10 foot long, and as big as ones Leg, placed over the great Boats side, one near each end of it, and reaching about 6 or 7 foot from the side of the Boat: By the help of which, the little Boat is made firm and contiguous to the other. These are generally called by the Dutch, and by the English from them, Out-layers. The use of them is to keep the great Boat upright from over-setting; because the Wind here being in a manner constantly East, (or if it were at West it would be the same thing) and the Range of these Islands, where their business lies too and fro, being mostly North and South, they turn the flat side of the Boat against the Wind, upon which they sail, and the Belly-side, consequently with its little Boat, is upon the Lee: And the Vessel having a Head at each end, so as to sail with either of them foremost (indifferently) they need not tack, or go about, as all our Vessels do, but each end of the Boat serves either for Head or Stern as they please. When they ply to Windward, and are minded to go about, he that steers bears away a little from the Wind, by which means the stern comes to the Wind; which is now become the Head, only by shifting the end of the Yard. This Boat is steered with a broad Paddle, instead of a Rudder. I have been the more particular in describing these Boats, because I do believe, they sail the best of any Boats in the World. I did here for my own satisfaction, try the swiftness of one of them; sailing by our Log, we had 12 Knots on our Reel, and she run it all out before the half Minute-Glass was half out; which, if it had been no more, is after the rate of 12 Mile an hour; but I do believe she would have run 24 Mile an hour. It was very pleasant to see the little Boat running along so swift by the others side.

—WILLIAM DAMPIER

As my companion, an old Englishman named Mr. Davis was selected.
He had lived on Palau from his childhood, had as a young man married a
native woman, and had so taken on the customs of the islanders that he was
everywhere considered an aborigine.

Mr. Davis with his large family felt very contented among his people;
no remembrance of his original home or of the main traits of European
culture remained with him. A very scanty knowledge of English was all this
strange man had left. At the beginning of our acquaintance I often sought an
opportunity to ask Mr. Davis for an explanation of this peculiar attitude,
but weeks passed before I succeeded.

"I don't want to know anything about England, Sir," he said crossly.
"I live here satisfied and happy—fish in the water, taro in the ground,
coconuts on the trees, warm sun and blue sky—enough for a man."

After that answer, I asked no more questions. Why should I disturb
the happiness of this man who was lost to civilization?

. . .

Our way led through a dense palm forest. Wonderfully rich vegetation held my attention. The fresh green crown of leaves sways at the top of a slender bare trunk, and from it the reddish-brown, ripe coconuts hang, while the young fruit with its cooling juice is modestly hidden among the leaves. Thick peppergrass surrounds the trunk of the breadfruit tree; its fruit, something like a pumpkin, hangs shining through the heavy foliage. Laboriously the betel palm works its way through the leafy vines; blooming bananas, pandanus, guavas, a mass of ornamental plants unknown to me complete the marvelous sight of this tropical profusion. Unfortunately this paradise lacks the heart-warming song of birds and the sounds of the animal world. During the day only the soft cooing of the green wild doves interrupts the mysterious quiet, and as darkness falls, there is the monotonous cry of a little owl. The flying foxes, also called kalongs, which spend the day hanging asleep in the trees, now flutter through the air like ghosts.

For some time we walked through this colorful forest; then the leader suddenly turned off the path. The laborious walk lasted barely ten minutes when we reached the edge of the woods. At the nearby shore a canoe was waiting which was fulled with a number of women; their skill in paddling brought us quickly to an opening in the rocks through which we reached a beautiful bay. Climbing plants with huge leaves, thick shrubbery edged the shore; white water lilies, brilliant vines shimmering in the bright sunshine lay nearer us. Branches of the lovely rabottel heavily laden with fruit dropped into the emerald-green water.

Even today that majestic picture stands as an entrancing vision in my mind's eye; I paid little attention to the lively conversation around me. Only the direct speech of the leader wakened me from my reverie.

—Captain Alfred Tetens

Pirates and sea dogs were becoming the unacknowledged agents of the Royal Society. The truth that was wanted, however, was novel truth, truths of far lands, new faunas, peoples, and customs. It was the truths of the world that were being sought. It would not be long before the remote latitudes penetrated by the mariners would transform these geographical inquiries into an even more surprising navigational adventure—the exploration of the past. Islands would become like upthrust remnants of vanished eons emerging from the old sea floors. Even this figure of speech does not entirely express the reality. Islands are genuinely different worlds. The pasts from which they take their origin have differed at some point from the biological history of the nearest continent and therefore the plant and animal life to be found upon these bits of land is marked by differences which are enhanced by the length of time they have been isolated.

One world, such as that of the Galapagos, may be marked by the emergence of giant turtles not to be found on neighboring coasts; another, like South Trinidad, may be dominated by land crabs; another give rise to peculiar flightless birds, of which the dodo in the Mascarene Archipelago was a perfect example. The entire continent of Australia, really a giant island long lost and disconnected from the great primary centers of evolution, constitutes, with its peculiar marsupial fauna, not a world of living fossils, but rather a world that has taken its own divergent way into the present.

—LOREN EISELEY

Considering the small size of these islands, we feel the more astonished at the number of their aboriginal beings, and at their confined range. . . . we are led to believe that within a period, geologically recent, the unbroken ocean was here spread out. Hence, both in space and time, we seem to be brought somewhat near to that great fact—that mystery of myseries—the first appearance of new beings on earth.

—CHARLES DARWIN

1. CANOE AND GALLEON

THE ISLANDS of the central Pacific, simple and sunny and open to the sky, have a curious second side, darker, full of allegory and obscure intention. It was this aspect that preoccupied Melville, mildly at first in the picaresque novels of his youth, and more fully later in the mystical novels of his maturity. Perhaps the ghosts and the meanings are palpable here because, with so little land to root themselves in, to rest on, they must hover. The island people, too, are beautiful but they have a melancholy, as Gauguin saw, and painted.

The three million square miles of Micronesia, an ocean within an ocean, are bounded by symbols. They wait beyond the edge, like the monsters that awaited Atlantic sailors when the world was flat. West is Tinian, the island from which the first atomic bomb was dropped on men. East is Bikini, the atoll evacuated of its people for the first hydrogen bomb test, and now, nearly twenty years later, habitable again, AEC scientists say. South is Nauru, where the islanders are busy mining themselves out of existence. When the people there have finished selling all the island's phosphates, Nauru will be a hole in the ocean with her reef around her. North is the desert of the North Pacific. If any latitudes of the biosphere approach being lifeless and void, they are these. The waters stretch away forever, pretty and blue, but empty.

So the islands are laid out like a lesson. Guam, like Tinian one of the Marianas, the westernmost chain of islands, is a lesson in itself. Guam's west coast is all highway, strip development, and huge military installation. This is one alternative open to the Micronesian people, who have like alternatives at all points of their compass. But Guam's interior is still jungle and savannah, wild enough to hide the Japanese stragglers who endured there until 1972, and who may endure today—the last straggler to surrender believes that some of his comrades remain—and watched from jungle hideaways as the jet bombers of a new war rose and flew west.

Guam's southern coast is still rural and calm. There

are breadfruit trees, and the coconut palms don't grow in rows. The savannah of the southern cape upthrusts here and there in small mountains of a kind unique to the Pacific. Like the mountains of Tahiti and the palis of Hawaii, the Guamanian hills are much too steep to be so green. The few houses below them were built by the hands of the owners and painted in gay colors. Above Umatac Bay, where Magellan first landed, in the middle of a long green ridge, a small cemetery's white headstones stand like seabirds just now settled. And farther south, beside a small roadside store, is the double arch of a ruined stone bridge from Spanish days, when galleons running between Manila and Acapulco paused to resupply.

Galleons were exotic ships here, built from a consciousness foreign to these waters. They were conveyances for earthly treasure, and they wallowed, like the great tankers that have superseded them and carry oil in place of gold. The native ships of these islands did not bludgeon the waves, but skimmed them. They were built from an entirely different idea about why men should sail. They were outrigger canoes, seldom more than thirty feet long, swift and acrobatic, and so light that when they capsized, swimming men could right them. The native seamen traveled about like water boatmen, the insect kind. They tacked by lifting the mast from one end of the canoe and carrying it to the other. When not working, the men hunkered on frail lee platforms and talked, or just watched the sea as it passed by, seldom faster than six knots. The canoes drew almost no water, and were perfect for an ocean full of submerged reefs. The canoes were small not because the Micronesians were unable to build bigger, broader ships. The potential for giant tankers resides equally in all peoples. But sometime in the earlier wisdom of the race, Micronesians decided not to go that way. Yes, went an unspoken consensus, our hulls might be made to overpower the sea, but why? What would be the point in that?

In the Caroline and Marshall islands there are still men

who sail outriggers. They prefer the simple, brave way. Ships travel regularly among these islands, and the islanders could travel as deck passengers if they wanted, but they don't want. Sailing is the great adventure and central joy in life. The people make up the feeblest excuses to travel hundreds of miles. "It would be a good time to go to Truk and get some tobacco," a master navigator decides; "I'm going to Pikelot!" a young man shouts, jumping up from among his drinking companions. "Who is coming with me?"

The prow of the galleon civilization clubs its way through history. It makes a hell of a splash, and measures its success by the height of the bow wave. The prow of the older civilization slips through cleanly. The older boat builders are as familiar with hydrodynamic principles as the new, and are experimenting as continuously with their hull lines, but all to make the canoe ride higher on the water. Their older society is not ideal. Its people are provincial in as pure a sense as is possible on this planet, and in their vast backwater they do not undulate with the great human movements of the continents, nor have they access to the great thinkers of any lands beside their own— an insularity that is both a strength and weakness. They have brutal caste systems and a history of savage wars; but so, of course, does the new civilization. If there is a difference between the two, it's that the older way is time-tested, having succeeded itself here for between one and three millenia.

Other things being equal, it would seem that the civilization that displaces least water is best. But it has been decided, apparently, that this is not so: that the success of millenia is of no account and the island cultures that passed on, through all those successive generations, the living reefs with their various and variegated fishes, and the green, fecund jungles, and the flawless beaches painfully white in the sun, must now give way to a civilization that can't pass a thing on intact, and has never learned to live harmoniously with anything, a civilization that in its short time here has killed the reef encircling Guam, among others.

It would be convenient if there were a man, a Viceroy-General perhaps, who was responsible for this decision, and could be confronted, and asked for his reasons, or even a group of men. But the decision was not reached in this way. There is no one to get angry at. In their present acceptance of the decision, the Micronesians themselves were party to it. It's tempting, for someone who believes that the decision was wrong, to be angriest at Micronesians. Was the new culture really so seductive? Did they need to renounce the three millenia so quickly, with so little regret? The new culture *was* that seductive, of course. Seductiveness is its distinguishing trait. Micronesians were, and are now, looking in at a windowfull of baubles, with all the price tags turned down. Their history, in which the only other men they encountered were powerless castaways, did not require them to develop a sense of competitive pride. When the galleon civilization arrived in strength, and it told the people that their life was inferior, they could think of nothing to say. They killed a few of their own Captain Cooks, but went about it with no real conviction.

The navigators of the central Carolines sail through a universe entirely different from the one Western men know. In the navigator's universe the canoe and the stars are fixed, and the ocean and all the islands in it flow past. This movement of creation is, at least, part of his scheme for finding other islands, and for the purposes of the system he thinks of things this way. He steers by dead reckoning, on hundreds of star courses memorized during his years of apprenticeship. He aims less toward a single star than toward the shape of the night sky. Thomas Gladwin, a visitor to Puluwat Island was baffled by the system until he learned this about the heaven's shape. How could two navigators of the island disagree about which star of a large constellation to use, Gladwin wondered, yet both reach their destination? Then he realized he was expecting more accuracy of the system than was necessary. Understanding came with a flash, like meteor entering atmosphere. It was a small flash, maybe, of a kind that commonly trails a mind as it crosses into an unexpected universe of thought. But such small flashes are one of the rewards of life on a diverse planet.

The Carolinean navigator holds his course in the daytime by maintaining the angle of his canoe across the waves. He does so as much by his feel for the waves passing under the canoe as by his eyes. He knows the direction of origin of the different kinds of waves he will encounter. He intuitively allows for the drift of the current, and reckons the distance traveled on each tack with a rough unit of measurement based on his intuition and on his scheme for the universal flow of things. When he feels he is nearing the island of his destination, he shortens his tack and looks for seabirds, following the birds in if it is evening, when they fly home from fishing, and in the morning sailing in the direction they have come. He uses a corroborative system, called "Sea Life," which asserts that on each of the hundreds of possible journeys between islands, certain sea creatures will be encountered, in a sequence unique to each journey. For the return trip the sequence will be reversed. That such sequences are not always observable does not bother the Carolinean navigators, who memorize them as carefully as they memorize star courses. Sea Life seems intended to quicken with mystery and life a system that, free though it is from devices, would be still too mechanical without it. Caroline-island navigation is very accurate. The navigator is at sea more in an inner universe than an outer, but he rarely gets lost.

The voyage deepens all experience. The fact of sex, at sea, becomes weighted with extra significance. In Micronesia when men and women voyage together they are careful that members of the opposite sex don't see them eliminate. This is not easy on a boat as small as an outrigger, and requires countless small pretenses. On calm seas women jump over the side and pretend to bathe. In rough seas a man pours water to mask the sound his wife makes. If a woman's time of month comes on a voyage, special precautions are taken. On the sea women become more mysterious.

There are small satisfactory things about life at sea. Coir rope, made by men in what otherwise would be idle moments by rubbing coconut fiber between palm and thigh, then twisting the strands together in cables and lines of varying thicknesses, has a peculiar bristle that makes tying knots unnecessary. A Micronesian sailor has only to lay a coir rope once over itself, and it will hold.

Such are the systems and sensibilities that around the world are falling to the galleon civilization. We need a word like "biomass" to suggest the weight of good ideas, innovations, systems of etiquette, God-understandings, insights, viewpoints, and small human graces that are being lost to mankind. The sheer ponderousness of what has lately vanished should have tipped the planetary scales and brought the whole thing down, and perhaps it will. But maybe the word is just "humanity." That's weighty enough.

What was it like for the Chamorro boy who chose to become a navigator, and was taken out to sea by his teachers? The Chamorros, the native people of the Marianas, no longer sail outriggers, but they once did. Sometimes a master navigator of those islands would ask his apprentice to leave the canoe and float free, to better understand the waves he was learning about. An outrigger canoe, responsive as it was to the waves, was considered to intervene too much, apparently. So the last artifice between the apprentice and his direct experience of the sea was gone, and he was alone in it.

Did his instructors take the apprentice out over the Marianas Trench? They must have.

The waters of the Trench are the deepest in the world. The sea creatures that die in the upper regions, to fall as a slow and steady organic rain, never reach the bottom. Long before that, they are intercepted by strange fish that become stranger, and fewer, the deeper they live. The deepest, waiting where darkness, pressure, and cold are most profound, are apparitions, with huge mouths and insubstantial bodies. The apprentice could infer much of this, for sometimes islanders found deep-sea fish dying on the surface. The swim bladders of the infernal fish were everted by the decrease in pressure, and protruded from their mouths, as if to tell the tale of the terrible weight of water under which they lived.

The apprentice felt himself suspended there, above the depths. The sun was warm on his face, and it warmed the waters about his chest and shoulders, but an abyssal cold welled up from below. The cold's progression was from pit of stomach to chest, like fear. The apprentice wanted to grasp the problem, to please his teachers, who waited in the canoe some distance away, hidden from time to time by the swell. Were they patient men, or stern? Both kinds, surely. The cold from the depths pulsed up—or seemed to pulse. The cold's diffusion upward is likely smooth and steady, and it is probably our senses that pulsate in recording it. It was coldest between his toes, anyway. Perhaps, as he rode that pillow of cold, fear of failure became confused with fear of the fathomless depths below.

But body accustoms itself quickly to ocean's cold, and in a few minutes the apprentice was comfortable in it. The sibilance of the sea was in his ears, the calmness, the assurance. The ocean filled and expired with him. What was it that his teachers expected of him? Was it simply a rhythm they wanted him always to remember, and were burning into him through repetition? Maybe it was with the last repetition, the final necessary undulation, that he understood, without quite knowing how. Or was it a complex problem of intuition and intellect, solved by inspiration? Perhaps for the first hours—or days, if the canoe returned more than once—the sea just felt like water under him. Then somehow the jumbled message of the waves sorted itself out. Suddenly the waves were speaking to him. We know what our own flashes of understanding are like, the little jumps of genius required to grasp a concept in geometry or natural science. But what is comprehension like when its instrument is the entire body, and the problem solved is the boundless sea?

Did he understand with his every cell? It may have been so. It may be that the skill of Micronesian navigators is possible only because man began in the sea, and as single-celled animal rose and fell, pitched and tumbled, with it.

Perhaps that was the connection the apprentice made as he floated there alone—a recollection. A door opened and his mind raced, at something like the speed of light, backward down man's perfect and uninterrupted succession from the sea, and inward into his particulate self. Perhaps his flash of understanding was *déjà vu*.

Whether the Chamorro apprentice made such a journey, or another of a lesser or greater distance, is a question that men can no longer answer. The particular experience of the Marianas navigator is no longer accessible to mankind. Fortunately, something very similar is still accessible in the Carolines and Marshalls, for now.

What is it like for the Palauan girl who undergoes the strengthening ritual that follows first childbirth? Today pregnant girls of the Palau Islands worry more about the ritual than about the pain of the birth itself. "But we do it because we know it's good for us," said one girl recently, a clerk-typist in a Koror government office who was about to have her first baby. "It makes us strong."

For a month after giving birth, a girl takes a medicine so bitter that some can't hold it down. For the first week afterward, she receives a daily scalding. She sits naked on a small platform of bamboo, its surface rubbed with coconut oil so that she can slide around a bit. Her body is rubbed with oil too, to mitigate the heat. When the pot of water comes to a boil, the girl spreads her legs, and an older woman tosses five cupfuls between them. A cupful is thrown at her face, with her eyes closed. Then she must open her eyes for a second cupful. For the full month of the ritual her body is stained yellow with a dye prepared from tubers of native ginger, grated, and mixed with coconut oil. Toward the end of that month, she must emerge from her confinement in a grass skirt and with breasts bare, whether she's a clerk-typist, of high clan, or what.

But how is it, after the ritual is over, when she sits with her new baby, the baby's skin against her own, now unbelievably soft and smooth from the coconut oil and hot water? What has she seen, staring into that second burning cupful? What has she learned about the nature of life and its creation?

One of the advantages in being born in a small place, and into a way of life unduplicated elsewhere on the globe, is that in a real way you weigh more than someone who is not. The four hundred people of Puluwat are not faces in the crowd. An infant born there is one four-hundredth of an entity, not a millionth or billionth. In a similar way, the islands themselves are vaster than they might seem. An

American reporter in Micronesia recently told the story of a chief from a small island who traveled to Guam for the first time, and was much impressed by that island's size. "Is the United States as big as Guam?" he asked. The reporter, who was amused, missed the point. The United States is not as big as Guam. Guam is something like the size of Asia and the Amazon drainage combined.

It is this weight of the people, and dimension of their land, that is threatened now as the symbols that lie beyond Micronesia's edge grow and impinge.

The notion that you can't fight the march of technology is common throughout the world, but it is especially strong in the young Micronesians who will lead the islands in the future. That man controls his destiny is a doubtful proposition to young people whose islands have been ruled by foreign powers for all their recorded history. Throughout that history, in which first the Spanish, then the Germans, then the Japanese, and now the Americans have governed, the only constant for the people has been their own powerlessness. Chiefs without real power became comic and sad. There have been exceptions—good and wise men, like Chief Petrus Mailo of Truk, whose personal force is too substantial to be compromised by his circumstances, or Judge Kabua Kabua of the Marshalls, who once let a group of young Hell-raisers off with a reprimand, except for his son, whom he sentenced to ten days in jail. But even these men have exercised their wisdom at the sufferance of one governor or another. With few models around for it, an ideal of heroic leadership is hard to come by. It's hard to imagine yourself as such a leader. In their uncertainty, young Micronesians are strangely inarticulate, for just as they have yet no great statesman to look to, neither have they had a great revolutionary thinker to call their own, and to give them a voice.

When Micronesian students arrive in Honolulu, where most of those who receive a higher education go, the first thing they notice is who is driving the cabs and sweeping up the airport. Hawaiians are doing those things, and white men are running the show. That's real education, and the students return to their islands with no illusions about who will benefit most from tourism there, or what tourism will mean to their land and culture. Yet they seem to find no fault in the kind of syllogism that H. Clay Barnard, the manager of the Royal Taga Hotel in Saipan, recently propounded: "I think that the island as it stands now in its sort of natural state is very beautiful and should not be changed, but by the same token you can't stop people from coming and if they come you've got to have hotels." Micronesia needs better logicians than that. The

last three hundred years of history seems to prove that you can't stop foreign people from coming, and Barnard's notion of progress seems to have the stamp of inevitability. But it need be only if Micronesians accept it as such.

There are a number of young Micronesians who are beginning to think of themselves as revolutionaries. They have a lot of harsh things to say about their rulers, but as yet few of them are questioning the basic direction imposed on their islands—the shape of the hull in the ruler's blueprints. A revolution that perpetuates the overlord's notion of progress is a funny sort of revolution. In Micronesia's classroom essays there is now much careless use of the words "forward" and "backward." There is much use of "inevitable," without an understanding of the power of that word itself. There is a confusion of the symbols of being Micronesian with the essence of being. *Thus*—the loincloths of the islands—don't mean Micronesian, any more than feathers mean Indian or Afros mean African. The basic precepts of the outrigger civilization are the thing—the shape of the hull. Islanders without that are just cigarstore Micronesians.

Today there is a steady flow of Micronesian youth away from the subsistence economy of remote villages and outer islands, and into the district centers. Children finish elementary school in their native place, then leave for high school and jobs in Koror, Majuro, Colonia and other centers, usually never to return. The young Micronesian leaders of the various O.E.O. programs and community action agencies, and a few in government, are alarmed at this movement, and they see what it portends. They know the limbo of the transitional culture that awaits immigrants to the district centers, for they are living it themselves. "But you can't tell that to the young people leaving Kayangel," says one such leader, a young Palauan woman of high clan, in reference to the abandonment of Kayangel, a remote atoll of her district. If she can't tell them, who can? Leaders should lead, not follow the people wherever they *seem* to want to go, but the old habit of generations of foreign domination is strong. Young Micronesians continue to migrate into trouble, into juvenile delinquency and identity crisis. Those who might divert the tide persist in regarding it as inexorable, like the tides of the ocean.

That young Micronesians invest this popular tide with the force of a natural phenomenon is odd, for they have uncovered evidence of how artificial it is. A group of radical Micronesian students recently published a secret introduction to the Solomon Report, a U.S. government analysis of Micronesian prospects. The introduction states frankly that the United States has no intention of abiding by its U.N. trusteeship agreement, by which Micronesia was supposed to be prepared for independence as soon as possible. The potential military importance of the Trust Territory of the Pacific Islands is too great for that, the introduction says. Then it outlines the steps that should be taken to move Micronesians out of their subsistence economy, in which they are self-sufficient, and into a cash economy, in which they will be dependent on the United States.

There is little reason to doubt that the secret introduction is genuine. The U.S. intent in the central Pacific has been clear from the beginning. The trusteeship agreement, drawn up when the United States dominated the U.N. as it does no longer, is a "strategic" trusteeship, the only one in the world. In explicit and unique language the agreement grants the United States the right to build military bases anywhere it wishes in the islands. There is no evidence that U.S. motives have changed since then. The United States has governed Micronesia for twenty-five years, and the people are still not free. The government has built, whatever its motives, a fake economy in which all but a fraction of salaried Micronesians work in the massive government bureaucracy. These men and women still know how to fish and plant taro, but soon they will forget, for subsistence skills depart quickly when not exercised. They will pass a point of no return, the point beyond which acculturation becomes a one-way street, and will find themselves irrevocably hooked on cash. Self-sufficiency will become a memory.

Perhaps it makes little difference whether the introduction is genuine: whether the fake economy is cynical, or is the work of men of good faith who are simply operating with the American bias about what direction is forward. (If there is a difference, it's that men of good faith, if their programs proved disastrous, would consider changing them, and cynical men would not.) Perhaps the secret introduction just provides a villain for a story that does not really need one. But genuine or not, Micronesians believe that it is. It is hard to find a Micronesian who is not convinced that a policy something like that outlined in the secret introduction is in effect in the Trust Territory. For Micronesians, the Solomon Report is a lesson in how the inevitable can be arranged. But they have yet to arrange some inevitability of their own.

The irony in all this is that of all the men in the world, Micronesians are perhaps the freest to shape their own destiny. There are few of them, and agreement about the path to follow should be simpler than for most peoples. The islanders have less to fear from their smallness than ever before. (The world's great military powers are answerable as never before, and at the same time, their need for island bases in the Pacific has lessened.) Micronesia is much more a potential liability to the United States than a military advantage, and in any debate over the shape of the prow the Micronesians have the whip hand, if they choose to take it.

Most Micronesians still live in a subsistence economy, and an arrested momentum lies there still, should they choose to resume the direction they were going before Magellan landed. Unlike most American Indian tribes, whose young people must now learn their tradition from books, the traditions of the various Micronesian peoples are living. They are handy for easy reference.

Micronesia has precedents for insisting on its own path. For guidance in this matter, islanders can go to the Yapese elders, who have declared the island of Rumung off limits to foreigners, or to the Ponapeans, who have resisted the construction of a new hotel so firmly that the developer has given it up. Micronesia has leaders waiting to lead. The combined population of the islands is that of a small city, but the men in the Congress of Micronesia look less like city councilmen than like statesmen. It seems likely, from the faces, that when nations are small and scattered, more men are called upon to be wise, and more men respond. Whether the men within are as strong as their faces remains to be seen, of course, but their ancestors were once, in days when they truly decided things. The men in the Congress cannot do that now, for a High Commissioner, a political appointee of whichever party is in power in the United States at the time, can veto any action they take.

It may be, of course, that Micronesians in the end will decide that the new civilization is best. Perhaps it's sentimental to worry about the outrigger civilization. Maybe it's mean, and unnatural, to feel a chill when a small brown girl, returning from Guam to her home island for a visit, says in the military-base accent, or absence of accent, *"Mommy."* (Then, having caught her mother's attention, she points out her plane window at the long, green island that has appeared in a featureless ocean since the last time she looked—her natal soil—and asks in excitement, of a place she can no longer recognize, "Is that Palau?")

One of the arguments against the outrigger civilization is historical. Times change, the argument goes; the fate of any civilization is to become something else again. The present diversity of man owes to the synthesis, in various combinations, of ideas and races that have been allowed some time to develop in isolation. Resisting that synthe-

sis is unnatural, and bound to fail. If there is an answer to this argument, it's that before now change has been evolutionary, with the old culture imparting some of itself to what followed it. But the galleon civilization brings with it a new kind of extinction, a kind that neither Roman nor Mongol brought. The galleon civilization keeps a few things that it finds cute. But for young people trying to define themselves, dances that endure to sell beer, and traditions animated by Disney, are worse than oblivion.

A second argument against outriggers has to do with accepting reality. It is the argument of many educated Micronesians and Peace Corps volunteers. They see all the dangers ahead if Micronesia goes Western. They agree that for Micronesia, so distant from world markets, a cash economy is unlikely ever to be more than a sham, dependent on an everlasting dole from some great power. The islands could sell their beauty, true, but would likely end up like women who do the same. The educated Micronesians and the volunteers see all that. Yes, they agree, a people whose only industry is tourism become poor imitations of themselves. Yes, the outrigger civilization would probably be best. But you have to accept the reality of the situation. "It's all very well to talk about self-fulfilling prophecy, but we live here, and we know the forces at play. We have to work here. Some things *are* inevitable. The people simply do not want the old way. Come to my class sometime, if you really believe it's possible to go back to the old life. Those kids don't want to fish or grow taro. The first thing they want is a cassette recorder, and after that a car."

So the educated Micronesians and Volunteers decide that their role must be to make the difficult transition as easy as possible. This makes for a strange and unhappy, but very common, phenomenon. A Peace Corps Volunteer, with a growing suspicion that his project won't help the people, begins it anyway, for he has only two years to accomplish something in, and before he leaves he very much wants to help the people.

This reality-of-the-situation argument is the hardest to respond to. It can be answered only with an article of faith: that man controls his fate. And most of the evidence seems to deny that. As to what Micronesian kids want, perhaps it's not so simple as cassette recorders. In every classroom in the Trust Territory there is a malaise about the direction the islands are embarking in, and a regret for what is being left behind. It's hard to find a student who is flushed with the American Dream. Their disquiet has simply yet to find a voice. Malcolm X once warned of the danger of being integrated into a sinking ship, but Malcolm X is not standard reading in mission

school. And Malcolm wouldn't do for Micronesia, of course. There needs to be a Micronesian Malcolm, an island flag to rally around, someone to cry out that the High Commissioner is wearing no clothes. Perhaps that's all that is needed to change reality.

The argument against the outrigger civilization that is easiest to answer is the one about "anthropological zoos." It is made by people for whom the only conceivable value of another culture is as a curiosity.

If the existence of the island civilizations needs to be justified, justification is probably in the islands' potential for otherness. The best thing about the potential is that it remains undefined. But potential for something.

Sometimes, in those moments when thoughts run teleological, it seems that this potential is what Micronesia's green islands, so supiciously like Eden, surrounded by temptations, are here for. Maybe the season the islands await is nuclear. It may be that seeds of the flower that opened above Bikini, and were scattered from there, will themselves flower, and bring the whole imposing edifice down; and that here in the middle of the Pacific, human seeds will endure, in the knowledge of how to survive without the edifice. Or maybe the crisis will be unforeseen, not any of those we imagine. Perhaps the islands are full of unpredictable significance, like mammals in an age of dinosaurs.

The islands do not require a crisis, though. They are valuable simply for their difference. It's in the fabric of a cheap world that the pattern repeats itself. In Micronesia the pattern is different. The islanders still have their own view of life and the world. Without that view, the collective body of mankind loses one of its senses.

In English class recently a Palauan boy wrote:

"Last night was windy night and also the coolest night that I have seen in my life. It was almost to make every people to obey their mind when they think of it. But it was true when we thought of it. I thought some people were dreaming of it when they were thinking of it. It would make them upset and broken hearted in their mind. That is why I mentioned these kinds of bad day in my life. It made me ill and upset and many kinds of bad dreaming."

It is hard to know exactly what the boy was trying to say. Whatever it was, he did not convey it successfully in English. Perhaps his idea was not utterable in English. Perhaps it was a Palauan idea.

At about the same time, at the other end of the Caroline Islands, another Micronesian boy, from the class of '74 of a mission school in Truk, wrote, "This idea of speaking the same language makes the students of Xavier High School forget that they are from five different districts of Micronesia. What a great gift from the Americans to solve the problem of unity in Micronesia!"

It was on the first day of March, 1954, that the hydrogen bomb was detonated at Bikini Atoll. The winds that day blew in a direction that had not been anticipated. Fallout from the test drifted over Rongelap Atoll, 105 nautical miles to the west, and enveloped also the twenty-three crewmen of a Japanese fishing boat, the *Lucky Dragon*. Contaminated to a lesser degree were the people of Utirik, another Marshallese atoll, and some American servicemen.

A Rongelapese named Billiet Edmond was at home at the moment of detonation.

"I was making morning coffee," Edmond remembers, "when I saw an object like the sun rising in the east. It started upward. It was very clear, stronger than the sun rising in the morning. I thought they had dropped the bomb outside our lagoon. Four or five hours after the flash we started seeing powderlike particles falling. It was white like powder, just like powder. When it fell on a damp part of the ground, it turned yellow."

John Anjain was out on Rongelap's lagoon when the cloud came. "I was in my canoe when I first saw the particles falling. I finally had to quit fishing because the particles got in my eyes. When I came back to Rongelap, the island was almost white. The powder covered everything."

Each year since the accident, a medical survey has been conducted on Rongelap. For its first fifteen or sixteen arrivals, the medical ship was greeted gaily by the island's inhabitants. There were several days of physical exams, X-rays, blood tests, pills, and urinalysis. It was a festive time of parties, movies, and baseball. The Rongelapese had received nearly a million dollars in exposure compensation. There were cars, though not much road to drive them on, and outboard motors, and gray-painted government housing, and a new A-frame church. There were nineteen cases of thyroid abnormality, most of them occurring in young people who were exposed to the radiation as children under the age of ten. Eleven of these had been sent to Guam or the United States for operations, and from several children the entire thyroid gland had been removed. Most Rongelapese accepted these things with a fatalism.

John Perry was one of those who traveled with the team to Rongelap for the fourteenth anniversary of the bomb. Of a given afternoon, Perry writes, "a small line may be forming around the X-ray or physical exam quarters. At a nearby house, women prepare local food for a coming party. Evening may bring a movie—the most popular item the A.E.C. brings each year. This year yet another intrepid Western gunslinger galloped across the bedsheet screen. . . . Due to projector problems, the gunslinger was soundless, but the action still prevailed in living color . . . many a badman bit the dust in a haze of silent smoke.''

The Rongelapese no longer greet the medical ship so gaily. They are beginning to suspect that the doctors are coming less to help them than to monitor them. "Guinea pigs,'' is the phrase that many Marshallese are now using. They are unhappy, too, with the amount of compensation. In 1972 Lekoj Anjain died of myelogenous leukemia.

Things have changed since Perry watched movies on Rongelap, but there is still something terrible in his account of the silent bedsheet screen. Perhaps it's that the screen has become the real thing in his description, and the audience insubstantial. You can't quite see the rapt faces watching, you can only guess at them. And the guess is awful—that the watchers have indeed parted with their real substance and like the movie are in living, South-sea-island color but soundless. Glandless, anyway. It's the suspicion that these poor island hicks grinning at the screen, so much like all the rest of us, probably think, despite some grumbling, that one million dollars—or two million—is not a bad price for their children's thyroids. It's the suspicion that like the Rongelapese with thyroid-hormone tablets in the pocket of his bright, new, exposure-compensation shirt, all other Micronesians, if the day comes when their islands fall to imitation of the galleon civilization, and all the varied cosmologies and mythologies—the stories of Aol, the first human being born on Yap, and of Uab, whose giant, fallen body became the Palau Islands, and of Medechibelau and how he halted the construction of the stairway to heaven by lighting a coconut husk and raising it in imitation of the dawn—when all these and all the proverbs and songs have been replaced by Western movies; and when Caroline navigators no longer steer to the Great Bird, the constellation that marks the east in their celestial compass, and trust instead to the magnetic kind; when cans of tuna at the corner store have replaced the bump-head parrot fish, big-eyed squirrel fish, goat fish, trumpet fish, milk fish,

rudder fish, porcupine fish, rainbow runners, wrasses, *mekebud, bolobel, kmai, ksull, emang, mejouk, ngali,* and *korali,* of dead reefs; and when the last spearman hangs up his spear, will then think they have entered the promised land.

It is a paradox of evolution that the people alive at a given time are but manifestations of their race, ghosts; and the real race is fleshless and bloodless, and resides invisibly in the genes. A race belongs less to its present incarnations than to the Past and the Future, a fact recognized in an elemental way by all organisms, by those fish that die in spawning, and by bulls that die fighting in the rut. It is recognized by men who teach their sons to cast a net or carve a hull, for just as surely as genes are bearers of the essence of a race, so is its culture. Both kinds of essence-bearer are at once obdurate and frangible, like diamonds.

The future of Rongelap still lies in the shadow of the cloud that drifted over from Bikini, though the cloud has long since passed. We can only hope that everything will be all right, that the deepest consequences of the Bikini radiation have now surfaced.

Of the other cloud adrift now in the Pacific, the one that changes cultures, the consequences are also in doubt. No precipitation of white ash accompanies this cloud, this agency, but it drives fishermen in from the lagoon just as quickly as John Anjain was driven in that day in 1954. Its presence is not detected by geigercounters or urinalysis, but by simply watching for Toyotas or Datsuns, or listening for transistor radios. Its absence can be tested too, very cheaply, with a fish spear, or paddle, or weighted casting net. The tester hands the net to an island boy. He watches as the boy spreads a single thickness of the wet mesh across his chest, like a bib, and gathers the rest of its weightiness in either hand. The boy waits, as intent as a wading bird, until a school of sardines shifts near enough, then his hands fly outward and apart, and the net, unfurling, floats out above the water. If the boy knows his craft, the net will fall in a perfect circle on the water. He has passed the test; the cloud has not yet arrived on his island. Fortunately, for all of us and for the fullness of our planet's texture, many of Earth's calm lagoons are still dimpled regularly by perfect circles.

...eluding the compass

"A person too early cut off from the common interests of men," Jean Rostand, the French biologist, once remarked, "is exposed to inner impoverishment. Like those islands which are lacking in some whole class of mammals." Naturally there are degrees of such isolation, but I would venture the observation that this eminent observer has overlooked one thing: sometimes on such desert islands there has been a great evolutionary proliferation amongst the flora and fauna that remain. Strange shapes, exotic growths, which, on the mainland, would have been quickly strangled by formidable enemies, here spring up readily. Sometimes the rare, the beautiful, can only emerge or survive in isolation.

—LOREN EISELEY

I saw on your walls this confusion of sunlit paintings that haunted me in my sleep that night. I saw trees that no botanist would ever find, animals that Cuvier never dreamed of, and people that you alone could have created.

A sea that looked as if it had flowed from a volcano, and a sky that no God could inhabit.—Monsieur, I said in my dream, you have created a new earth and a new sky.

—AUGUST STRINDBERG, *Letter to Gauguin*

Banana trees, Sokehs Island, Ponape

I tried to work, making all kinds of notes and sketches.

But the landscape with its violent, pure colors dazzled and blinded me. I was always uncertain; I was seeking, seeking. . . .

In the meantime, it was so simple to paint things as I saw them; to put without special calculation a red close to a blue. Golden figures in the brooks and on the seashore enchanted me. Why did I hesitate to put all this glory of the sun on my canvas?

Oh! the old European traditions! The timidities of expression of degenerate races!

—Paul Gauguin

She was not at all handsome according to our aesthetic rules.

She was beautiful.

All her traits combined in a Raphaelesque harmony by the meeting of curves. Her mouth had been modeled by a sculptor who knew how to put into a single mobile line a mingling of all joy and all suffering.

I worked in haste and passionately, for I knew that the consent had not yet been definitely gained. I trembled to read certain things in these large eyes—fear and the desire for the unknown, the melancholy of bitter experience that lies at the root of all pleasure, the *involuntary and sovereign* feeling of being mistress of herself. Such creatures seem to submit to us when they give themselves to us; yet it is only to themselves that they submit. In them resides a force which has in it something superhuman—or perhaps something divinely animal.

—Paul Gauguin

Mother and child, Pisaras Island, Truk

Among peoples that go naked, as among animals, the difference between the sexes is less accentuated than in our climates. Thanks to our cinctures and corsets we have succeeded in making an artificial being out of woman. She is an anomaly, and Nature herself, obedient to the laws of heredity, aids us in complicating and enervating her. We carefully keep her in a state of nervous weakness and muscular inferiority, and in guarding her from fatigue, we take away from her possibilities of development. Thus modeled on a bizarre ideal of slenderness to which, strangely enough, we continue to adhere, our women having nothing in common with us, and this, perhaps, may not be without grave moral and social disadvantages.

On Tahiti the breezes from forest and sea strengthen the lungs, they broaden the shoulders and hips. Neither men nor women are sheltered from the rays of the sun nor the pebbles of the sea-shore. Together they engage in the same tasks with the same activity or the same indolence. There is something virile in the women and something feminine in the men.

This similarity of the sexes makes their relations the easier. Their continual state of nakedness has kept their minds free from the dangerous preoccupation with the "mystery" and from the excessive stress which among civilized people is laid upon the "happy accident" and the clandestine and sadistic colors of love. It has given their manners a natural innocence, a perfect purity. Man and woman are comrades, friends rather than lovers, dwelling together almost without cease, in pain as in pleasure, and even the very idea of vice is unknown to them.

—PAUL GAUGUIN

Under the continual contact with the pebbles my feet have become hardened and used to the ground. My body, almost constantly nude, no longer suffers from the sun.

Civilization is falling from me little by little.

I am beginning to think simply, to feel only very little hatred for my neighbor—rather, to love him.

All the joys—animal and human—of a free life are mine. I have escaped everything that is artificial, conventional, customary. I am entering into the truth, into nature.

One day I put my tools in his hands and a piece of wood; I wanted him to try to carve. Nonplussed, he looked at me at first in silence, and then returned the wood and tools to me, saying with entire simplicity and sincerity, that I was not like the others, that I could do things which other men were incapable of doing, and that I was *useful to others*.

I indeed believe Totefa is the first human being in the world who used such words toward me. It was the language of a savage or of a child, for one must be either one of these—must one not?—to imagine that an artist might be *a useful human being*.

—PAUL GAUGUIN

The light was dim, and after the brilliant sunshine for a while he could see nothing. Then he gave a start. He could not make out where he was. He seemed on a sudden to have entered a magic world. He had a vague impression of a great primeval forest and of naked people walking beneath the trees. Then he saw that there were paintings on the walls. . . .

"What was the subject?" I asked.

"I scarcely know. It was strange and fantastic. It was a vision of the beginnings of the world, the Garden of Eden, with Adam and Eve— *que sais-je?*—it was a hymn to the beauty of the human form, male and female, and the praise of Nature, sublime, indifferent, lovely, and cruel. It gave you an awful sense of the infinity of space and of the endlessness of time. Because he painted the trees I see about me every day, the cocoa-nuts, the banyans, the flamboyants, the alligator-pears, I have seen them ever since differently, as though there were in them a spirit and a mystery which I am ever on the point of seizing and which for ever escapes me. The colours were the colours familiar to me, and yet they were different. They had a significance which was all their own. And those nude men and women. They were of the earth, and yet apart from it. They seemed to possess something of the clay of which they were created, and at the same time something divine. You saw man in the nakedness of his primeval instincts, and you were afraid, for you saw yourself."

—Somerset Maugham

2. A NEW VOYAGE

THE *Hoi Kung* is a freighter in the small fleet of ships that serves the Trust Territory of the Pacific Islands. She is 360 feet long, with a gross tonnage of 4454.55. She was commissioned in 1964, and was originally rigged to run Chinese between various ports of Asia. She carried 900 deck passengers. On her forward deck is a row of the huge rice boilers that fed the Chinese, now used for storage. None of the ship's present officers was with her in those days, but Hans, the Chief Engineer, recently left a ship with a similar mission. That ship ran Moslem pilgrims from Bangkok to Jeddah. In the beginning, Hans says, when a pilgrim died the ship's Captain made a little ceremony of stopping and committing the body to the sea, but soon they were running far behind schedule. After several days at sea the bodies were just dumped over. When the ship arrived in Arabia there were exactly as many passengers as had started out, the births balancing the deaths.

So the Joseph Conrad days in these seas have never ended. The *Hoi Kung* is a new ship, with modern nautical equipment, but the view from her bridge, down to decks where 900 people somehow found room to sleep, and lined up at mealtimes before the boilers waiting for their rice, cannot have been very different from what Lord Jim saw.

The ship is now chartered by Micronesia Interocean Lines to carry freight between the west coast of the United States and the ports of the Trust Territory. It is not a profitable run, and the ship may well return someday to her old business.

The *Hoi Kung* is as friendly to allegory as the *Pequod* was. As on Ahab's ship, the inhabitants of the *Hoi Kung* are of many races. Her officers are Norwegian, her stewards Hong Kong Chinese, her passengers for the most part elderly Americans, and her crew Micronesian. Since "Micronesia" is just a convenience for cartographers, and embraces a number of very different islands and peoples, the crew is more correctly Marshallese, Ponapean, Trukese, Chamorro, Yapese, and Palauan. There is one crewman from Kapingamarengi, an island culturally part of Polynesia but politically part of Micronesia's Trust Territory. Painted on the *Hoi Kung*'s stack is the emblem of the ship line, a circle of six white stars against a blue field. Each star stands for a district of the Trust Territory, a cluster of islands. As microcosm for Micronesia, the ship is not quite perfect. It would be better if the officers were American. The allegorical significance of the Chinese stewards is puzzling, if indeed there is any. A whale to chase would help the story, but there is none. The ship's voyages are without climax or satisfactory conclusion, and the fate of the voyagers is left in the air. Yet perhaps that is appropriate to a place where the future is so much in doubt.

The passengers spend their days on the boat deck, sitting or reclining on foldable furniture. They read mysteries, or sleep. They burn, peel, and freckle in the sun. Aft of the passengers, separated from them by the valley of the central hold, are the crew's quarters, outside which the Micronesians who are off duty sleep on woven mats, or sit on coiled hawsers. They talk, or stare out to sea, or with downcast eyes regard the deck while a fellow crewman cuts their hair.

The attitudes of the voyagers change little, from day to day. On the boat deck the smallest passenger, a baby girl, plays in her crib. Her father sleeps in a lounge chair nearby. The baby will be taken in soon, but the father, if he holds to his daily custom, will stay in the sun for hours longer. His lobster-red skin has exhausted its power to peel. The red simply deepens briefly, in protest, after each exposure. The father is a San Francisco hairdresser. He knows that too much sun is bad for him, but he hates his pale winter's face, and lying in the lounge chair he fights his battle against it.

At the very stern of the ship a Micronesian sleeps. He lies on his back in the shade, for at this stage of his life more sun would be superfluous. He is dark enough already. Under him is a piece of cardboard that he uses for a mat. His feet are turned outward, his hands folded on his big stomach, and his heavy, stubbled face is in repose. Tied to the railing above his head is a trolling line. The line runs out into the ship's wake, where the lure bobs to the surface now and again, chasing the ship. Nearby lies a second Micronesian, a younger, smaller, and more fastidious man. He is clean shaven, and sleeps in plaid shorts on a woven mat. His head rests on a tiny pillow, placed exactly at the mat's center. The dark, raised welts of his burn marks—Micronesian men and women of several districts pledge their love by burning themselves with cigarettes—lie in a perfect row on his upper arm. Both men sleep soundly. If a fish had hit the trolling line, neither would have known about it.

The passengers are mostly retired people who discovered freighter travel late in life, and now spend much of their time at it. There is Howard, a retired brigadier general who was in biological warfare research during the world war. He has spindly legs, a wide waist, a thin, brown, World War II Colonel's mustache, and small Nazi eyes. He smokes large cigars. Later in the voyage, in a port of the Marianas, Howard will see a Japanese fishing boat, its masthead unashamedly flying the rising sun, tied up next to an American LCT. He will be infuriated. "They let them dock there like that?" he'll ask, appealing to the heavens and the passengers around him. The tall photographer, Wenkam, will look at the general in amazement. "But the war's over," Wenkam will say. "We won!" The general will fall silent, to suck in frustration on his cigar.

There is the Canadian couple, both born on the prairie, where they spent hard lives. They are weary now, and amenable to any argument. The general's position makes sense to them, and so does Wenkam's.

There is the small man from southern California who plucks viciously at his wife under the dinner table whenever she says anything, hissing at her, his face contorted by rage. She often leaves the table in tears. When the Californian is not harassing his wife, he is suspiciously watching Wenkam, who sits next to him. He waits for Wenkam to knock something else over with one of the wild, expansive, conversational gestures of his long arms.

There is the old Danish gentleman who owns a papaya plantation in Hawaii. He is eighty years old, the oldest of the passengers, yet the wittiest. He is a brave punster, and a proposer of beautiful toasts. He is never drawn into shipboard feuds, and he alone of all the passengers has nothing bad to say about his fellows. He is tolerant of the imperfection in the others. He seems even to appreciate the imperfections.

There are several passengers who join the ship along the way. Three Army wives embark at Guam. The three are ill at ease, and seek one another's company. They are all traveling without their husbands for the first time, and perhaps they are uncomfortable in that. It seems likely, from their whispered conversations and other evidence, that each is debating whether to admit to her cabin the ship's wolf, one of the Norwegian officers. Each decides against it, with some relief, apparently.

There is the somber American girl from the loveliest atoll in the world. She and her husband have been contract teachers on one of the islands of the atoll's broad circumference. They were both Midwesterners, and both from Calvinistic sects, his the more antediluvian. For months at a time on the island he did not touch her—whether from religious conviction or from aversion to her she could not tell. She would walk alone to the island's ocean side to watch the sunset. When the sunset faded on the ocean, she would make the ten-minute walk across the breadth of the island to the lagoon side, where she watched the moonrise. The moonlight on the lagoon's calm waters was so beautiful she could not believe she was there. She asked her husband, again and again, to watch with her and finally he consented. He spent the sunset throwing rocks at crabs. She is leaving him now, to start over again.

Among the crew is the Yapese sailor who left Yap as a young man and has spent sixteen years at sea to earn the money to buy a store in Yap, so that he can return to Yap again. There are the four Chamorro boys, Ben, Tony, Joaquin, and Phillipe, who keep a stash of marijuana concealed in their cabin. Each afternoon, when they have finished their shifts, the Chamorros shut the cabin door and begin their evening ritual. They winnow the marijuana, roll, light up, and pass it around. As the room fills with smoke they grin at one another, content and unworried, secure here, observed only by the big ship's roaches that skitter along their walls.

Somewhere between California and the Marshall Islands, a passenger decides he knows the *Hoi Kung* as well as he knew his crib, or the climbing tree in his backyard. Every brass knob, every cabin door, every face is familiar. The virtues of each deck chair have been weighed, and a favorite picked. All the books on the two shelves of the ship's library have been handled, and several have been read. Then, strolling the deck one night, the passenger looks in through a porthole to see the galley for the first time. It happened so for one passenger, at least. The passenger looked in. The Chinese cooks and stewards hunkered there, beyond the steamy porthole glass, eating with chopsticks from bowls of rice and fish. They wore shorts and T-shirts cut differently from the Western kind.

The ample neck openings of the shirts exposed much collarbone, and seemed to give the stewards plenty of room to breathe. The sleeves were longer than the Western kind. They reached down the slim stewards' biceps almost to their elbows. The material was a very thin cotton that looked as if it should feel good against the skin. Somehow it was the T-shirts that made this unexpected country, glimpsed through porthole glass steamily, so strange.

In this unexpectedness of the galley the ship was indeed like the world, full of new corners for jaded passengers. The passenger turned from the porthole and resumed his walk. A ship is like the world also, the passenger decided, in that a lesson seems to hang above the voyage, never quite to be grasped. Sometimes the lesson seems simply to be that, like all ships, this is a ship of fools. Sometimes the lesson seems to have to do with destinations. It is difficult, sailing on a tropical ocean at night, to believe there is a destination. Or that the enterprise makes any sense. The passenger reached a stairway, and climbed to higher decks.

Standing at the rail of the boat deck, looking down from its height at the night sea, he felt the ship under him. Forward was the dim figure of the officer on watch, who was dressed in his whites, and had just stepped out on the bridge to flip a cigarette into the sea. The officer looked for a moment at the stars. Then he returned to the wheelhouse. The deck was deserted again.

The ship was not so wide that the passenger, looking forward, couldn't see the foam, struck from the sea by the wedge of the ship's prow, slide by him to port and starboard. His peripheral vision caught both foam margins at once, and they streamed away whitely at the corners of his eyes. The ship's few lights illuminated only this water disturbed by the ship's passage. The lace of foam was ghostly, partly reflected ship's light and partly phosphorescence. Waiting beyond the edge of the lace was a lightless ocean, and out there, except for an occasional glimmer as a small wave broke on itself and caught the light, everything was black. The ship's milky margins were reassuring in the night, but only a little, as the galaxies of the known universe are reassuring. Aware that he was on a vessel, and was proceeding into darkness, the passenger took his elbows from the rail, and strolled aft. He paused at the ventilator shaft to the engine room, and looked down. The tremendous heat rising from the shaft was a shock after the balmy night wind. The passenger blinked his eyes to remoisten them. Far below him was the pit of the engine room. As nearly as he could judge, the engines labored beneath the level of the sea. Leaning over the shaft, the passenger's head had entered a column of noise suddenly harsh and tympanic. Elsewhere on the ship the sound of the engine was muted, and was so engraved on a voyager's consciousness, waking and sleeping, that he heard the engines only when they changed speed. Now, in the blast of heat and noise, the passenger felt himself looking in, as if through a door accidently opened to him, at a secret furnace, at the heart of the vessel, its moving principle.

There was a catwalk around the engines, along which a shirtless Micronesian walked, oiling the rocker arms. He gave the working parts of each arm squirts of oil, in a fast, unvarying sequence, and he repeated the sequence for each of the eight arms. The Micronesian was a young man with wild hair and a beer belly. Or maybe it was a taro-and-fish belly. He moved mechanically down the row of pistons, like a machine himself except for the evidence, in his hair and stomach, that he was at least in part a sensual man. The passenger could not decide how to interpret the Micronesian. Was the task of tending the engine hopeless, and was the crewman Sisyphus? Or was he, with his wild hair, someone like Prometheus, full of promise and hope? The passenger, in watching the sequence of lubrication, found himself strangely hypnotized. He shook free of that, and strained to reach a decision. He could not. He waited for the Micronesian to give some other sign. The Micronesian gave none. The man finished his oiling, and passed from sight.

...still haunting the mind

Those who try to be artists use, time after time, the matter of their recollections, setting and resetting little coloured memories of men and scenes, rigging up (it may be) some especial friend in the attire of a buccaneer, and decreeing armies to manoeuvre, or murder to be done, on the playground of their youth. But the memories are a fairy gift which cannot be worn out in using. After a dozen services in various tales, the little sunbright pictures of the past still shine in the mind's eye with not a lineament defaced, not a tint impaired. . . .

There is an isle in my collection, the memory of which besieges me. I put a whole family there, in one of my tales; and later on, threw upon its shores, and condemned to several days of rain and shellfish on its tumbled boulders, the hero of another. The ink is not yet faded; the sound of the sentences is still in my mind's ear; and I am under a spell to write of that island again.

. . .

The inimitable seaside brightness of the air, the brine and the iodine, the lap of the billows among the weedy reefs, the sudden springing up of a great run of dashing surf along the seafront of the isle, all that I saw and felt my predecessors must have seen and felt with scarce a difference. I steeped myself in the open air and in past ages.

There was another young man on Earraid in these days, and we were much together, bathing, clambering on the boulders, trying to sail a boat and spinning round instead in the oily whirlpools of the roost. But the most part of the time we spoke of the great uncharted desert of our futures; wondering together what should there befall us; hearing with surprise the sound of our own voices in the empty vestibule of youth. As far, and as hard, as it seemed then to look forward to the grave, so far it seems now to look backward upon these emotions; so hard to recall justly that loath submission, as of the sacrificial bull, with which we stooped our necks under the yoke of destiny. I met my old companion but the other day; I cannot tell of course what he was thinking; but upon my part, I was wondering to see us both so much at home, and so composed and sedentary in the world; and how much we had gained, and how much we had lost, to attain that composure; and which had been upon the whole our best estate; when we sat there prating sensibly like men of some experience, or when we shared our timorous and hopeful counsels in a western islet.

—Robert Louis Stevenson

No alien land in all the world has any deep strong charm for me but that one, no other land could so longingly and so beseechingly haunt me, sleeping and waking, through half a lifetime, as that one has done. Other things leave me, but it abides; other things change, but it remains the same. For me its balmy airs are always blowing, its summer seas flashing in the sun; the pulsing of its surf beat is in my ear; I can see its garlanded crags, its leaping cascades, its plumy palms drowsing by the shore, its remote summits floating like islands above the cloud rack; I can feel the spirit of its wood-land solitudes, I can hear the plash of its brooks; in my nostrils still lives the breath of flowers that perished twenty years ago.

—MARK TWAIN

Kiti mangrove swamp, Ponape

Usually when he smelled the land breeze he woke up and dressed to go and wake the boy. But tonight the smell of the land breeze came very early and he knew it was too early in his dream and went on dreaming to see the white peaks of the Islands rising from the sea and then he dreamed of the different harbours and roadsteads of the Canary Islands.

He no longer dreamed of storms, nor of women, nor of great occurrences, nor of great fish, nor fights, nor contests of strength, nor of his wife. He only dreamed of places now and of the lions on the beach. They played like young cats in the dusk and he loved them as he loved the boy.

—Ernest Hemingway

The house was painted white to be cool in the summer and it could be seen from a long way out in the Gulf Stream. It was the highest thing on the island except for the long planting of casuarina trees that were the first thing you saw as you raised the island out of the sea. Soon after you saw the dark blur of casuarina trees above the line of the sea, you would see the white bulk of the house. Then, as you came closer, you raised the whole length of the island with the coconut palms, the clapboarded houses, the white line of the beach, and the green of the South Island stretching beyond it. Thomas Hudson never saw the house, there on that island, but that the sight of her made him happy.

—ERNEST HEMINGWAY

After Ulithi comes the long haul to Woleai and it is at this point
that one begins to feel oneself amidst the Outer Islands and the field
trip routine—meals, boats, copra loading—sluggishly asserts itself. And,
in retrospect, it is at this point that memories of the islands begin to blur.
All—with the exception of Fais—are low and small. Heading for shore, you
feel that you are not really stepping on land, but rather that you are boarding
another ship, a floating raft covered with sand and coconut palms,
permanently anchored in a huge sea. On one side of the island is a village,
there is seldom more than one; to the left and right the trail wanders off
into coconut groves and taro patches and the backsides of the islands are
lonely and deserted. A visitor's walking tour ends early and—sooner than
he'd expected—he finds himself back in the village, seated in the shade of a
coconut palm or in a boat house. . . . A visitor sits and looks—offers
cigarettes, is offered a coconut, exchanges words and stares, sticks his head
in a church, strolls to the cemetery—there's very little variation in the
routine. Yet, against a background of flat islands and thatched houses, out
of the smell of cookhouse smoke and buzz of flies, from a long gallery of
remembered faces and bodies, from the feeling beneath one's feet of sand
beaches and coral paths, springy swards of short-bladed grass and wood-
shavings in boat houses, out of this procession of scribbled notes and
contrasting moods, some memories—sharp and specific—do emerge.

. . . the afternoon brightened and Ifaluk, which had been colorless in the
morning rain, soon flashes grassy lawns, high green palms and imposing
boat houses—tall imposing slopes of thatch, with fish nets spread on the
surrounding grass to dry, giving the whole scene the intricate, measured
beauty of a formal garden. And suddenly the whole population appears:
the men crowding around the ship's boat and the women, much more
reserved, sitting further back in groups, minding babies, passing cigarettes,
and staring at visitors. As each of the boats come in, the villagers
converged on the beach, crowding around, and when the boat left again, the
assembly scattered back in groups under trees. With every boat they came
together, with every departure they moved back beneath the palms, and that
was the rhythm of the afternoon, until the last boat left, with waving and
wailing for the villagers who were leaving Ifaluk.

—P. F. KLUGE

Today is a great day to fish. On my island, we usually go fishing when the rain is really falling hard. The fish go tame under the rain.

That's why I want to be on my island just for today. I want to be with the boys of my island school because I know some of them are fishing this morning for meat for the school's dining hall. They always go out in the rain in the morning to fish.

—Kino S. Ruben

Its voice is always in the ear, sometimes subdued and wooing, sometimes as murmurous as the slow breathing of a sleeping beast, sometimes as wild and clamorous as a battle cry. All other sounds—the calling of birds, the wind over the heath, the speech of men—are flute notes against the deep orchestration of the sea.

Here the people seem to possess the secret of tranquillity and to live lives of more than surface contentment. That is rare today. Perhaps it is only by going up the old back roads leading to the lost little hamlets of the mountains or the seagirt islands and peninsulas of the world that you can still find it. . . .

—LOUISE DICKINSON RICH

Nan Madol, Ponape

3. TWELVE ANGRY MEN

ST. XAVIER HIGH SCHOOL occupies what was once the Japanese communications center for the central Pacific. The Japanese designed the building for war. Its concrete walls are three feet thick, its windows equipped with heavy steel shutters. Its two stories stand on a high point of land on Moen Island, and overlook the minor sea that is Truk's lagoon.

Bishop Kennally sits in the school office, writing letters. The leaded panes of his window look down on the school's playing field, a green rectangle cut from the jungle, and below that the sunny ocean. Kennally sits in a handmade wooden chair, rudely carved and stained by his students. Around him are bookcases, their shelves stacked in no special order. Theology and fiction are mixed together with Jesuit mission reports. A painting of Pope Paul and several crucifixes hang on the wall. There is a wooden head of Christ on his desk, and numerous mementos. Above the desk is the school insigne. The insigne, like the office, is full of things. A blue unicorn with a golden horn stands on a black plain. In one hoof the unicorn holds a sword-cross of gold. Above the plain is a light-blue sky, and in the sky a dark blue moon, with crescent moons to either side. These and several other symbols all stand under the protection of a green Bishop's hat and rosary. An inscription beneath reads, "The Islands Put Their Hope in the Lord."

It is Saturday, and the school is quiet. The schoolboys are in town, or across the way in the dormitory building. From somewhere within the main building comes the tinny sound of a phonograph. There's also the sound of a basketball. Bishop Kennally's office opens on a balcony above the lofty, dim and cavernous room used for a gym, and someone on the floor below is bouncing one. Only one boy is playing, from the sound of it. It's a one-boy rhythm. Bishop Kennally is an old man who for decades has lived among boys, and for him the sound of the basketball, and the phonograph, and the occasional voice raised in mild Saturday-afternoon argument, is as good as silence.

The solitary basketball player is a Yapese boy named Clement Mulalap. Clement plays guard on the Xavier team. He has good speed, and scores most of his baskets on fast breaks, but now he is practicing free throws. The sweat shines on his chest and shoulders.

The gym is very hot. Its concrete walls cut off the hilltop breeze, and the heat builds through the day. No one

plays basketball for long. Yet for some reason the pick-up games are always full-court. Some younger boys enter and join Clement in a game. One boys acts as referee, shouting "Other way!" if an offensive player loses the ball out of bounds, and "Same way!" if a defensive player last touches it. The court has no boundaries besides the walls of the gym. Sometimes the ball bounces out the doorless doorway, or out the glassless window. A boy runs to retrieve it; a pleasant task, for it's much cooler outside in the breeze. Sometimes the ball rolls under a raised stage that abuts the court, and must be fished out with a stick kept handy for that purpose. The play gets ragged very quickly because of the heat. Weaker boys wilt. On Moen they have never heard of playing half-court. It would be a good and humane introduction to the island.

In the game Clement Mulalap seems something of a straight-arrow. When the referee makes a bad call, Clement does not protest. The referee is a younger, smaller boy, yet Clement just grimaces and turns the ball over wordlessly, as if there were a fine for complaining. He is serious and quiet, a lightskinned and handsome boy, with chiefly features and the full Yapese jaw. His best subjects are history and English, and he wants to become a lawyer.

Clement's manner is troubled. There is often a cloud where his brows meet. He worries about the future, which is being billed as a totally different proposition from what has gone before in Micronesia. It is hard to guess what such a future will be like. Clement is not sure how a lawyer will fit in. He worries too about college in California, where he will almost certainly go soon. His uneasiness is shared by many boys at Xavier, who all must try to imagine a future for which neither their island backgrounds nor their present education unsuits them. Clement is perhaps a little more tentative than most. (He is playing in the gym alone on a day when most of Xavier's boys have gone to town. There is frequent trouble between the young Trukese townsmen and the Xavier students from other islands, and Clement chooses to avoid it. Sometimes, after lights are out in the dorms, Xavier boys sneak out and walk to town, but Clement has never taken the chance.)

It was this year that Clement felt himself pass a point of no return. During the summer vacation he did voter-registration work in the outer islands of the Yap district, and he found the life there alien and strange. He was happy to return to Xavier. He is presently somewhere in between, like the castaway who has pushed off from the safety of his drifting log, hoping to make it through the reef to land.

Above in the office, Bishop Kennally looks up for a moment from his writing, and sees a distant white ship against the blue of the ocean, the *Hoi Kung* making her way toward his island.

That night the students of St. Xavier High School present a play, "Twelve Angry Men," at Mizpah High, a mission school in town. The play is held in an outdoor cafeteria, where rows of foldable chairs have been set up. The few white people in the play's audience—some teachers and several passengers from the ship—seat themselves as soon as they arrive. The Trukese do not. A great crowd of them stands outside in the darkness, smoking and conversing, and looking in at the Americans, some of whom feel peculiar, seated so sparsely amidst empty rows of seats. Just before the play begins the Trukese move in and sit down.

The play is on the deliberations of an American jury. Clement Mulalap plays one of the angry jurymen. Drama is one of Clement's interests, and he does a good job. He is cast well—as the juror who keeps saying, "Let's be civilized." Clement is not nearly so effective, though, in spite of the good casting, and for all the sensitivity and introspection of his private life, as is the Marshallese actor who plays the angriest man. The Marshallese is a dark boy, with a hoodlum's walk and a topknot like the young Floyd Patterson's, and it is he who fixes the attention of the audience.

The Micronesian accents of the American jury are heavy, and the man who is supposed to have come recently from Europe is as dark as an African, yet the Americans in the audience suspend their disbelief, and so do the Trukese. The play is in English, so it is doubtful that the Trukese follow the plot perfectly, but they appreciate the drama. There are snickers when the black boy says, improbably, "When I came from Europe . . ." At the funny lines, white teeth flash in the darkness. Sometimes there is laughter in places that seem inappropriate, but it is laughter to relieve tension.

The one uncomfortable moment comes at the play's end, when the actors troop out in threes to make their curtain calls. The Trukese are unfamiliar with the custom. Clearly there is something in Trukese tradition that makes such a gesture wildly vain, or otherwise improper. An audible embarrassment runs through the audience. Only the Americans clap. The embarrassment quickly infects the cast, but the show must go on, and they continue to file out by threes to bow. The embarrassment climaxes in the final bow by the entire company. At last the ritual that by now, even to the Americans, seems insane and interminable, ends, and everyone is released from his agony.

Umatac Village, proposed Guam National Seashore

Songs from Ifaluk Atoll

Rain did not feel cold to me, for it would do the taro good.
Sun did not feel hot, for it would make the plants grow.

. . .

The soil is rich there,
We used to enjoy making things grow.
Here we would plant taro, and there angorik,
In that rich soil they came up fast;

The tall taro shaded us from the sun.
We worked until we were tired out,
Then rubbed angorik over our faces and shoulders
And started for home.
The angorik pleased all who passed us.

. . .

After leaving the taro swamp,
We would sit down to rest on the way,
For the walk was tiring after our day's work.
We would talk a while longer,
Then come on home.

Back home, she would say, "Look, mother, how nice I am!"
And I would laugh and answer, "Yes, you are lovely!"
The sun would make her perspire
For it was very hot,
But she would let the perspiration stay,
Running down beside her eyes.

Yapese girls dancing, Maap Island

He lies down on his mat,
Thinking of his canoe,
How well fashioned it is.
He is full of canoe-making lore,
He forgets none of it.
Are you skilled in the craft? Good!

His father taught him how to build canoes.
He stands beside the hull,
Puts a new loincloth and young white
    coconut leaf over it,
Ties young banana leaf on his arm,
Wraps a piece of it about his waist,
Puts paint on his face.
All who see admire him.
He makes a wreath of coconut leaf for his head.

He understands adz craft,
He chops skillfully,
Working on the outside of the hull;
He shapes the keel,
Grasping the adz firmly.
He remembers to work fast,
He wants to have the canoe finished,
He forgets nothing of his craft.
Some people gossip about him,
But it does not worry him.
Boy, never mind what they say!
Remember how to manage the lashing,
And pay no heed to the talk.
You are like the flower in my hair.

. . .

He is making the canoe for his own use,
He prepares pandanus leaf to give it speed,
Folding it between thumb and first finger.
The keel is of breadfruit wood,
He lays the pandanus leaf against it,
And along the cutwater;
He passes along the hull,
And lays strips of leaf where it broadens out.
He brings a feast for the workmen
And prays to the gods to enter him,
Semerik and Seilangi.
There is only a little work left to do;
The god gives strength to his arm.
He hews the lines well and truly.

—IFALUK

4. FLYING FISH

THE BERTH is narrow and painted white. Its long walls recede, in exaggerated linear perspective, toward the porthole at the end of the room. A small white writing table has been folded down from beneath the porthole, and is locked in a working position. Squarely in the center of the table sits a blue Olivetti portable typewriter. At eye level above the Olivetti is the heavy glass of the porthole, and around the glass at intervals are big naval rivets, painted white. To one side are heavy white hinges, and to the other oversized white wingscrews, which when twirled counterclockwise allow you to swing the round window open, and let in the sea breeze.

All these are constants of a rectangular universe in perfect order. What changes is the ocean that the porthole frames. The berth is on the port side. When the ship rolls to port, the line of the horizon climbs upward until it disappears, and the sea entirely fills the window. The circle of ocean is either stormy blue, when skies are dark—and it is then often flecked with rain—or bright blue in the sun, but is always, under any sky, laced with foam from the ship's passage.

When the ship rolls to starboard, the ocean horizon drops away, pushed down by the sky, until sky alone fills the circle.

Sometimes a flying fish, breaking from the bow wave and fleeing the ship, moves into the circle. It travels something like a dragonfly, maintaining the same narrow distance between itself and the swells. One fish darts from the bow wave. It breaks past the lace of foam, flies twenty-five yards across the deep blue, and enters with a surprised white splash the side of a wave. Another fish, stronger perhaps, its wings backlit by the sun, flies across the blue and into shining silver in the direction of the sun; a hundred yards, two hundred yards, still aloft, passing finally into the burning column of ocean directly in line with the sun, where it disappears in brightness.

When the ship comes to anchor in its various lagoons of call, there is no roll at all. The horizon stays still. The ocean beyond the porthole then is stratified. There is the turquoise of the shallow water within the barrier reef, and the dark blue of the ocean beyond it, and between the two blues, demarking them, a white line of surf breaking on the reef.

When the ship lies at anchor here, close by a low, tropical island, it is clear how much of the world is water. Except for the thin slice of land, the world outside the porthole is entirely made of that element, in its various densities. Above the three strata of the ocean, the sky is ever changing, full of trade-wind cumulus, incipient rain, that moves steadily past. Watery sky and ocean are forever in motion, streaming by at different speeds, with the island steady against it, like a ship against the current.

The island is flowing away also, of course, in a geological sense, and only seems fixed, like the moon when you drive through trees. But how good that relative solidness must have been after a long voyage in an outrigger canoe.

When, from the rail of the ship's bridge, the long and low island of Tinian first appears, it is a ghost of the horizon line. Considerable time must elapse, and considerable intervening ocean pass, before one can be sure Tinian is really there. A strong wind blows from the quarter, sending whitecaps toward the ship, and the canvas of the canopy above the bridge flaps briskly; yet somehow, despite the distance of the island and strength of wind, the sweet green smell of land finds its way through. In the approach to Tinian, as to other islands, there is a fresh amazement in the strength of that smell. Were Micronesian sailors amazed each time they smelled it? What was it like, down nearer the water, when the flapping canvas was a woven sail, and the world was not framed by a porthole? How sensitive were noses, after being at sea for periods that really amounted to something?

My husband is like the sweet-smelling ais,
Like the flower in my ear.

When he is living ashore
He cannot wait to be off again.
Every little while he gets up to study the night sky.
He keeps waking up, he is so eager to go.
The god of navigators descends on him,
The god Werieng alights on him;
Then he can sleep no longer.

He goes down to the beach
To gaze at the western sky.
At sunset he can tell tomorrow's weather.

He could not sleep at night.
As I lay by him, he said, "I must go away."
I have no heart for work,
I lie and think of him,
I think, "If only he could have stayed."

I think of my beloved gone to Yap.
While my body sleeps here, can I go to him in a dream?
Can I go to him like rain falling?

I don't want to see anybody else;
I see others going about but he is not there;
He is far away.
If he were only here so I could see him!
Only the sight of him would delight me.
I am weary with longing.
Along the path that leads to our house,
My husband might come.
I don't want others to use it.
Just before he went, on a hot night,
After going out to cool himself in the breeze,
He came back and talked to me.
"When I go, don't let anybody else come to you.
Whoever entices you, pay no heed.
If they say, 'Leave him, he is gone,'
   refuse them.
Tell them to stop their talk, send them away."

But in my heart I love him only.
I do not heed someone who speaks from the woods.

I am always thinking of him.
For a while I forget, then suddenly remember.
I have not put him out of my heart.
It is long since I saw him.
How handsome he was,
With his finely curved eyebrows
And dark glowing eyes.
I cherish his memory;
If he is dead, what shall I do?
Who could ever take his place?
News of his death would be a heavy blow.
I am afraid of the sharks
That gather about canoes at sea.

The canoe is carried into the sea.
They load it with food at its mooring place.
He longs to go, yet hates to leave his wife.
He must leave her, his flower, behind.
His fragrant leaf of angorik.
She cannot go with him
Because she has no baby;
If he should take her along, storms would come.

He gets to the captain's post.
Standing up on the platform,
He waves a branch over one shoulder,
    then the other,
Then lays it on the canoe,
And ties a piece about his neck.
He goes through the ritual gracefully.
Next he takes an aro branch
And waves it to bring him wisdom.
He takes the conch horn in his hands,
For he wants the crews to make haste.
Eight canoes will make the voyage,
The others following him.

The navigator recalls his sea lore,
Remembers the guiding star for Ifaluk;
When one is down, another rises.

He remembers those stars
Deep within him,
Stars by which he can steer
And grows impatient to be on his way.

Can it be that my strong son is dead?
He had a mighty arm.
No one is left like him
For a friendly word and a helpful hand.

In the lagoon he stood up in the canoe
And nobody could stand like that.
He came in paddling fast,
Lifting the paddle high,
Waving it over his head
From side to side
To signal his success
To the people on shore.

As he tore along through the water
His paddle made a sucking sound,
As if a flock of white terns
Were calling, there in the water.

. . .

Often he cruised about in the lagoon,
Visited the uninhabited islets,
Paddled over the reef nearby.

Then, leaving that part of the reef,
He would go to a favorite place of his
Where great loose rocks are piled on the reef.
He turned them over, looking for fish.

So he wandered about the lagoon,
For he loved to go fishing there,
In the nooks where the fish hide.

Leaving the rock-strewn reef at last
He would set out for home,
Paddling fast, as always.
The hot sun
Blazed down on his tattoed back
With its rich black designs
In colors that never fade,
In spite of sun and sea and rain.

He had done his work fast.
I would look out and see him,
With his fine black eyebrows,
The salt crystals on his shoulders,
And his flashing eyes.

. . .

So he came home from his fishing.
I would see the canoe coming.
See the flashing paddle,
And he would come ashore
And go to the canoe house.

Then he would come on home
Walking along the sand,
Telling of his luck on the way.
He would come to the meeting house
And tell everybody there
Whether he had fish enough to go around.
"I caught plenty this time,
The canoe is full of them."

Flower in my ear . . .
Like the fragrance of ais blossoms . . .
My precious ointment.

—IFALUK

Boy with fish, Pisaras Island, Truk

5. COLONIA

THE *Hoi Kung* leaves the blue sea for the narrow, greenish waters of a channel through the fringing reef. Within the reef lie the green hills of Yap. At the mouth of the channel, caught on the coral, is a rusty LST that went aground in the typhoon of 1952. The *Hoi Kung* passes very close to the wreck. When she is inside the channel her engines change pitch and she proceeds dead slow. Passengers and crew look down on the reef that edges the channel, sliding past very near. The water over the plateau of the reef is so shallow that the coral heads, widely spaced on the sandy bottom, are as clearly visible as clumps of sage in the desert. A Norwegian officer points back to the hulk of the LST, under which the coral grows solid, a rampart against the sea. The officer tries to convey how it is to leave such a wreck and cross sharp coral without proper footgear. His English is not up to it, so he gestures, suddenly smashing one hand into the other and grinding it, then widening his eyes, as explanation.

The shores of the island are continuous green mangrove forest. The mangrove trees soften the edges of all the landforms, and from deck it is impossible to tell islet from peninsula, or inlet from river mouth. Yap is a pleasantly modelled island—not monotonous, like the long plateau of Tinian, nor mountainous, like the islands of Ponape and Truk. Yap is somewhere in between.

When the ship has anchored in the lagoon some distance from the town of Colonia, a floating dock is pushed out by an LCM and made secure. Yapese longshoremen come aboard. The longshoremen all wear *thus*. They swarm over the ship. An elderly passenger emerges from her cabin just as six longshoremen, all short, dark-brown, muscular men with bright red lips, turn the corner of the narrow bridge deck. Startled, the passenger presses herself against the bulkhead to let them pass. Betelnut-stained lips are a Yapese feature, as inevitable as two eyes and a single nose, but they take a while to get used to. Each of the six men smiles in passing, to reveal a red liquid film over his teeth, as if someone, out of sight around the corner, had hit each man in the mouth before he came into view.

A Yapese boy of about twelve has come out to watch the unloading. He's a big boy, in a red and blue *thu*, with skin still smooth and childish except on his roughened knees, and here and there on his arms and legs, where he has the scars, in different stages of freshness, that mark anyone who lives without clothes in vegetation. He is handsome, with the broad, Afro-Oriental face and robust jaw of his island. He wears his hair in a natural, somewhere between wavy and nappy, and indented all the way around by a *maramar* of interlinked pop-tops from soft-drink cans. He stands, his long betelnut bag under his arm, on the tread of a caterpillar tractor that has just been offloaded. He studies the controls.

At dusk the longshoremen quit work and go home. Night advances, and the island as it goes black becomes more substantial. Its profile heightens. The waterfront lights come on, and they beckon. The LCM returns for those passengers and crewmen who want to spend a night on the town. Everyone crowds around the LCM pilothouse, and the boat heads in toward the lights. The four Chamorro boys stand together at the rail, full of smiles. Tonight they plan to buy enough marijuana to keep themselves loaded for the rest of the voyage, and they are going now to meet their connection.

In Colonia everyone stops first at O'Keefe's. Until recently O'Keefe's was a club for Americans, but now it is open to all. None of the voyagers stay long, for the club is slow tonight. Several Yapese sit at the bar. Two couples share a table near the jukebox, rising now and then to dance. Three Peace Corps volunteers—Mike, Richard, and Steve—sit at another table, drinking whiskey-sours, this week's alternative to the boredom of beer.

The three volunteers are all a bit blue. They have very little to say—it seems that in past evenings at O'Keefe's they have exhausted most topics of conversation. When

they do speak, it is with the special, wry, self-effacing Peace Corps humor. Their tone changes for a moment, and they talk with concern of a Peace Corps girl on the island and her bad luck, but suddenly they shy away, as if that were too much like gossip, and they have a compact about gossip. The table falls silent. The silence has a peculiar intensity, morose and incestuous. It seems to enjoy itself, grimly. The volunteers have seen too much of one another, and know it, yet they seem bored in the presence of anyone else. Of the three, Richard is the most animated, and Steve the least. Mike is the most thoughtful.

It's Mike's birthday, but no one knows it. Mike is newest to the island, having come to Colonia two weeks before from Lamotrek, an outer island of the Yap District, 500 miles to the east. His decision to leave Lamotrek had been hard. He liked the people, especially the children. He learned from them, and he planned to raise his own kids the way they do on Lamotrek—really listening, and paying attention to them. But he had hated his job on Lamotrek—he taught English there by rote. He asked to be transferred to Colonia, where he could do something else. He left without telling the people of Lamotrek he would never return.

So Lamotrek has been a defeat, of sorts. Mike has had only two weeks to get used to that, and tonight it's his birthday. He debates telling his friends about the birthday. Finally, with a little embarrassment he confesses it. His tone is not wistful, really. But Mike appreciates that, after the recent turn his life has taken, a birthday nobody knows about is supposed to be bleak, lonely, and full of irony. He dismisses that now by making mocking allusion to it, and affects a joking braveness in the face of it. And yet, silent again, he is not sure he doesn't feel some real irony, and a real need to be brave.

A white man enters with a Yapese girl. Richard watches the couple cross the floor. He turns to Mike

"Have you noticed that you can tell the Seabees from the Coastguards?" he asks. "The Seabees are big and sloppy. The Coastguards are skinny and neat."

Mike watches as more of Yap's Seabees and Coastguardsmen enter, and it's true. You *can* distinguish them this way. The servicemen are all in civilian clothes, but Mike already knows which branch each man is from—the service contingents on the island are very small—and he can see that the system works.

"And the Peace Corps," Mike adds. "They have steel-rimmed glasses and hair too long."

"And no girls," says Richard.

Mike is impressed by the truth of this. Here sit the three of them, with no girls. Richard advances his theory for why. Peace Corps Volunteers, Richard says, are so sensitive and so culturally aware, because of their Peace Corps training and because they have been to college—are so anxious not to break some unknown taboo—that the native girls get bored. The Seabees and Coastguardsmen could care less about the culture, and they chase the girls, which is what the girls like, of course. The sailors get the girls. Mike and Richard watch now as a callow and skinny Coastguardsman dances with his date. She looks a little away from the sailor, as if finding him slightly distasteful. He dances with no sense of rhythm whatever, and the two volunteers comment on this. Then they laugh at themselves bitterly.

A big, wide-hipped, unshaven man, who according to the formula should be a Seabee, enters, and Richard and Mike, who are facing the door, both groan. "There's that son-of-a-bitch," Richard says. Steve turns slowly to see who it is. The big Seabee walks to the bar and orders something, then begins looking around the room.

"Look," Richard says. "He's giving us the—of course he is—he's giving us the peace sign, the bastard." The Seabee is holding up two fingers in the direction of their table, while his head and eyes finish their sleepy circuit of the room.

"He's leaving Thursday," says Steve, looking dismally into his glass.

"He *is?*" Mike asks. His inflection starts to rise, but tails off immediately, reserving his happiness for the day the departure actually occurs.

At the center of the room a Yapese man in a short-sleeved shirt dances alone. The man dances innovatively, with humor, but not with his whole spirit. His eyes roam the room. Each time a girl passes him, on her way to the bar or the restroom, the man breaks off suddenly to follow her. He talks earnestly in her ear. Sometimes he reaches out to touch her shoulder. The girl pays him no attention. At most she smiles vaguely. A slight twist of her shoulder is enough to dislodge his hand. The man, who is the tour guide and the mechanic whose semaphores bring the planes in and the forklift driver during the unloading of ships and the all-night dancer at O'Keefe's, resumes his dancing. He is called Doublecheck, and he is considered one of the two insane people in Colonia.

Doublecheck gets his name from his habit of assuring people that everything is fine, checked and double-checked. "Check!" he says, holding up the O.K. sign. "Double check!"

Doublecheck might as appropriately be called "A Man Need a Woman," for this is his other habitual expression.

It's the fragment of a song he hoarsely gives voice to, from time to time, apropos of nothing. "A man need a woman . . ." he sings, ". . . a woman need a man." The song can't quite be apropos of nothing, for Mike, sitting in O'Keefe's and watching Doublecheck dance, knows when it's about to come. He anticipates Doublecheck, and softly begins the song a second before Doublecheck does, in perfect imitation. Together they sing a very brief round.

Doublecheck is fifty-one, but looks younger. His perpetual motion has kept him in trim. Doublecheck has traveled, and besides the two dialects of Yap, he speaks languages of all the other districts of Micronesia, as well as some Spanish, German, Okinawan, Japanese, and English. He has been married four times, and is the father of many children. For ten years he was fire chief of Saipan, the story goes. In school he went no further than the second grade, which was as far as a Yapese could go under the Japanese. He learned all the rest on his own. He was once sent to a mental institution, but was found sane and discharged. The theory among O'Keefe's Peace Corpsmen is that Doublecheck is a casualty of Micronesia's transitional culture, if indeed he is a casualty at all. He has traveled too widely, and seen too much of other worlds, they think, to be content on a small island.

Richard, who has been staring in Doublecheck's direction, seems to see him now for the first time. He watches Doublecheck for a moment, then tells the story of a Peace Corps girl—the girl of the bad luck—who was walking home one night when Doublecheck began to accompany her. She tried to stop at a friend's house, to shake Doublecheck off. "Why are you trying to get rid of me?" Doublecheck asked her. "Because frankly you scare me right now," she said. "All right," said Doublecheck. He turned on his heel and walked away.

Now Doublecheck abruptly stops dancing, picks up his betelnut bag, and strides out the door. He seems bound for an important destination, yet in five minutes he is back in the bar again, dancing.

It is not hard to guess what he found outside. There was nothing out there he didn't know the smallest detail of. There was the street of coral sand and coral dust. Across the street was the weathered theater, showing an ancient movie with Errol Flynn and Olivia de Havilland. Down the street and around the corner was the Yap Cooperative Association store. Beyond was the dock, then the lagoon, and finally the ocean. Doublecheck likely walked down the deserted street a way, singing, "A man need a woman. . . ." He stopped and looked around him. Then he turned and strode back toward the bar.

At midnight those crewmen who have no friends on Yap and have found nowhere to sleep on the island gather at the dock to catch the last LCM out to the ship. They are joined by the ship's four youngest passengers, the hairdresser, his wife and baby, and a single man, who have been at O'Keefe's and the YCA bar. The departure of the LCM is delayed, for no one can find the pilot. It begins to rain. The downpour is sudden and tropical. Most of the crewmen take shelter in the pilothouse of the LCM. The passengers and the four Chamorro boys stand together under the corrugated awning of the warehouse. They stand very close, hemmed in by waterspouts that empty to either side, pelting the ground. The hairdresser holds his tough, sunburned baby girl. The baby cried a little when he ran with her through the rain, but she likes it fine in the crowd under the awning. The forced closeness, and the awning's coziness under the tropical rain, and the alcohol everyone has drunk, and the friendly baby, make for brotherhood. The Chamorro boys ask the passengers if they smoke weed. Yes, the passengers do. The passengers should smoke some tonight, then, the Chamorros say. Ben, who at nineteen is the oldest of the Chamorros, a short, heavy, forever smiling Saipanese, confesses that they failed to buy any marijuana tonight. They will get some tomorrow, for sure, he says. But there is still some left from Saipan. The passengers arrange to join the Chamorros in the crew's quarters, and share it. "Very good stuff," says Ben, with a wink.

The rain slackens, and as it does Doublecheck appears. He is very drunk. He carries a bottle of a yellowish alcoholic mixture, with which he postures and gesticulates. He runs through the alphabet of a sign language of his own design—probably an off-duty elaboration of the semaphore code he uses, when sober, to bring in taxiing planes on Yap's small airfield. The sign language employs much sudden and wild use of his arms. Doublecheck rants for some time, until the ship's assistant radioman, a big, black Palauan named Moses, becomes weary of it and tells him to shut up. Moses is Doublecheck's friend, and the posturing embarrasses him. When Doublecheck persists, Moses loses patience and yanks him by the hair from behind. That hurts Doublecheck's feelings, and makes him angry. He protests that he was just trying to help. He was trying to solve the problem of the missing pilot. It looks for a moment as if Doublecheck and Moses will fight. But Doublecheck is not that drunk. His friend Moses is a very strong Palauan.

The agent for the shipline drives up in his jeep, having searched unsuccessfully for the missing pilot. He takes this opportunity to load Doublecheck into the front seat and drive him off. As Doublecheck departs he and Moses exchange curses, in several different Micronesian languages.

The dock is quiet for ten minutes. Then the people gathered there hear Doublecheck's voice in the distance.

"A man need a woman . . . a woman need a man."
He is returning on foot from a new direction. He strides into view. The walk seems to have sobered him somewhat. He and Moses shake hands, and tousle one another's hair, to show that yanking hair is no big insult.

The pilot arrives at last. Everyone piles aboard and the LCM pulls away from the dock, leaving Doublecheck alone with his bottle.

When the LCM reaches the ship, the baby is asleep in her father's arms. The hairdresser and his wife excuse themselves to put her to bed. They ask the Chamorros to smoke without them. So the four Chamorros and the last passenger walk aft to the crew's quarters. They shut the door, gather around the small table and light up. The Chamorros all grin. They love the idea of dope. They love talking the dope talk. Tony, making his eyes as if slowed down by marijuana, though it's a little soon for that, keeps saying, "I tell you, man, this is real good stuff." He speaks with what he imagines as a slowed-down American dope drawl, but it's thick with his Chamorro accent. It is not really very good stuff, in fact. Joaquin inhales, and nods indulgently toward another young Micronesian, who sleeps, or pretends to sleep, fully dressed on one of the cabin's six bunks. "He," Joaquin says at last, when he has exhaled, "doesn't smoke." Most outer-island boys are afraid to smoke marijuana, Ben says. To the passenger, the sleeping Micronesian seems to have the right idea. The passenger himself is tired, and the marijuana has no effect. It only makes him sleepier. He excuses himself and goes to bed.

The next morning early, Doublecheck's voice sounds from the side of the ship. Today he is tour guide, and he has come with two small boats to take the ship's passengers to Maap. Maap is one of several islands, separated by narrow channels, that occupy Yap's tight lagoon. Doublecheck promises Native dances there, and the passengers climb in. Doublecheck drives the lead boat. As he steers he continually bails, with a clorox bottle that has been cut into a scoop, and as he bails he jerks regularly on his trolling line to make the lure jump, and yet he manages to keep in constant communication with the following boat by arm-signal code. From time to time he reels in his lure to check the aluminum foil of which he has fashioned it. A passenger loses his hat, and Double-

check shifts the outboard to neutral, dives over, and swims for it, though he could as easily have steered back to it, picked it from the water, and stayed dry.

In the shallower places the coral heads are visible against the sandy bottom, and they race under the boat surprisingly fast. Something in the motion of the waves against the boat, or in the distortion of the water, makes it seem that the bottom is passing too fast. The coral heads speed at the boat and vanish behind, and the eye senses an illusion. The effect is vaguely unsettling, like walking on an escalator. The two boats thread the channel between the big island and Maap. Emerging from the channel, they turn right and coast along Maap's beach. Seaward, above the turquoise of the lagoon water, above the white line of surf that marks the reef, above the deep blue of the Pacific, a rainstorm advances. As the lowering rain cloud descends, it obscures first the deep blue of the Pacific, then the white line of surf breaking on the reef, and finally only the lagoon remains. The world narrows to turquoise. A mist of rebounding rain makes the lagoon's farther waves ghostly, and brings the horizon in close. The boats move through a small ocean of lagoon-blue. It's the wrong color for an ocean, but pretty—perhaps it's the right color for the ocean of a smaller, less serious planet. The first drops strike the boat, and pock the water around it. After the heat of the sun, the drops are very cold. Hearts beat faster, suddenly, and lungs draw deeper with the shock. The sensation is like fright. But in minutes, when bodies are all wet, they adjust and are comfortable again. One passenger—the young man who the night before did not like Saipanese marijuana—dips his hand idly in the water and discovers to his amazement that it is warmer than the air. The rain's cooling him has made the differential the more striking. The lagoon water is more than warm, it's almost hot. Moments later he dips again, and is surprised again. For a man whose seas have been northern, this warmth of lagoon water is the hardest thing in the tropics to come to terms with. It violates basic rules. For Doublecheck, of course, the warmth is no surprise. That's the way lagoons are. Now, as the rain flattens the lagoon's surface, he reels in his line for the last time, and places it at his feet.

Later that afternoon Doublecheck returns with weary passengers. They are all burned, and a little sick from the sun. Several are disgruntled, for the Yapese dances were not up to their expectations. The start of the performance was delayed, for the schoolchildren who danced had to make their costumes first. They put aside their lessons and ran with machetes to the edge of the schoolyard to gather broad leaves, to be shredded for their dresses, and flowers for their hair, and bamboo staves for the stick dances. These preparations had taken an hour, and the passengers saw no charm in them. They complain. Doublecheck listens, but his English, which fails him at convenient times, has failed him now. He has trouble understanding.

When Doublecheck has returned his charges to their ship, he adjourns to O'Keefe's for a drink. In the sandy street outside, he passes Robert Thomas, the architect for the Yap District, who has just closed up shop and is heading homeward. They nod at one another. Usually Thomas covers the distance between the Community-Development bungalow, where he works, and his house on an old, black, three-speed bike, but today he is walking.

Thomas is a Peace Corps Volunteer. He is bearded and bespectacled, of medium height, with a scholar's breadth of hips. He has white teeth, free of the dark-red betelnut patina that marks the smiles of most Peace Corps men and women on the island. It is hard not to chew in Yap. It is a habit that all Yapese begin early, and Volunteers find chewing helpful in bridging the gap between cultures. (The Peace Corps personality, too, seems simply to have an affinity for the habit.) In this Thomas is different, though he makes no virtue of it. Thomas is fairly happy with his work on Yap. Before coming here he did some graduate work in architecture, but he had no job experience, and on Yap he is trusted with responsibilities he would never have at home. Because of his position, and his beard, and a certain gravity of manner, and perhaps also because it's hard for Yapese to tell the age of Americans, some islanders take him for a man of fifty, and this pleases him. He is twenty-three.

Today Thomas takes the long way home. He passes O'Keefe's, the theater, and the post office, as usual, but as he enters the jungle at the far side of town he steps off the road. There the road's hard sand is met by a narrow, cobbled path that curves off into the forest. The path will loop inland, then back again to his house, which stands near the road he has just departed. Thomas sets off.

A walker need only step off the Colonia road to leave the society of the district center behind. It's a giant and magic step. Once a walker takes it, he has crossed to an outer island. There is no pathside junk, and no clue as to what century the path curves through. The pavement's squarish stones have been worn smooth by generations of bare feet, but are of irregular height, and it is easy in zoris to stub toes. Thomas now must watch his feet. On either side stands the forest, humid and neat, like a tropi-

cal conservatory garden of which the glass has been carefully shattered and carted away. The sunlight still falls muted, as through a glass dome. The close-growing trees and plants stand serene in the softened light. That a secret and skillful gardener has been at work here is not all illusion, for this is managed jungle. It's human country. The forest's slenderer tree trunks are those of coconut palms, and the slenderest are betelnut palms. Here and there stand breadfruit trees, and wetland taro grows in shallow ponds everywhere. Some of the ponds, planted to giant taro, are so small that they hold only four or five plants. The larger ponds are connected by thin irrigation canals, and the water level in each is regulated by small earthen dams, but neither canals nor dams are obvious. For someone new to it, Yap's interior seems just orderly jungle.

Thomas, moving through a dark part of the wood, comes upon a woman washing clothes. She works below the stone path, scrubbing in the trickle of a stream. She is dressed in a skirt only. She looks up as Thomas passes, and they nod at one another. She smiles. They exchange the Yapese greeting. "It was a pleasure meeting you." He continues down the path, and she returns to her wash.

For Robert Thomas, walking Yapese paths is not entirely pleasurable. This path is pleasant, for it loops through the domain of his adoptive clan, but elsewhere he is unsure of ownership, and of his welcome. In a letter to his girl friend, Thomas tried to explain the feeling. It was being like a guest at your aunt's house, he wrote. You were not free to arrange your own meals and hours. You felt appreciated, but not free to explore the upstairs, or to poke around in closets. The roads in Yap were not public in the way they were at home, and it was easy to offend people by trespassing. Perhaps this was partly why Thomas, in his early months on Yap, spent his free time exploring, pushing inland past the present areas of habitation to the abandoned villages of the interior, and beyond. In his wanderings he came to know the terrain of the island better than most Yapese, or so his Peace Corps colleagues claim. He knows where the war's ruined tanks rest, overgrown by jungle, and where the ancient house platforms are, the proprietary rights to the old stones fuzzy, or no longer at issue, and trespassing no offense. He can find the stone backrests against which the chiefs of Yap's grander, more populous past leaned as they talked, and decided things.

Today Thomas's thoughts have run to bicycling, perhaps because he is bikeless, having this morning left his bike behind. His father introduced him to bicycling in Pennsylvania and Delaware. He has been remembering. On a ten-speed bike you could do twenty miles per hour

in Pennsylvania, when you felt like it. On a weekend you could comfortably cover sixty miles in a day. From bicycling in that part of the country he knew five or six counties very well. Your shores were not constricted. There were no boundaries you couldn't cross. Now, in Micronesia, as he walks homeward down a path of fitted stones, Thomas remembers the bike path in Roosevelt State Park. He travels that path in his memory. Roosevelt Park follows an old canal. The canal is unused, but all its bridges have been preserved. He remembers the Park as about fifty yards wide, a little wider at intervals where it broadens to accommodate park tables, and at least fifty miles long. Then he recalls Winneseca Park in the middle of Philadelphia. There are deer in Winneseca Park. The Park can actually support a population of deer, in the middle of the city. That amazes him now. He wonders how it could have failed to amaze him before.

Thomas arrives at the cluster of houses in which his adoptive family lives. He speaks briefly with Tamag, the family head, then retires to his own small house. Leaving his zoris inside his door, he steps in bare feet across his plywood floor. The floor is clean and bare. Thomas's floors are nothing like the floors of the house where his colleagues, Steve and Mike, live, on the edge of the mangrove swamp at the other end of town.

In that house the floors are littered. Paperbacks and *Sports Illustrateds* are scattered about. Canned foods, pipes, pipe-cleaners, and clothes spill out from shelves. A small, very tough puppy roams about, tugging on things. The back door opens on the confusion of the mangrove swamp. Outside the door, a porch has been built above the swamp. The puppy sleeps there, in a cardboard box padded with old shirts. A faucet stands over a hole cut in the porch floor. Excess water from the faucet splashes through the hole and into the brackish water beneath. A square of mesh has been tacked over the hole so that puppies, school rings, eyeglasses, and other items will not fall through, to be lost forever to the swamp. From the edge of the porch a narrow plank runs out forty feet through the dappled sunlight of the mangrove forest to the *benjo*. The benjo is poised on mangrove stilts several feet above the water, and is flushed by each ebb tide. It is private only through a happy arrangement of the mangroves around it.

At bedtime Steve gives his guest, if there is one, the guest pad, on which innumerable former visitors have sweated away hot nights. No blanket is necessary. As Steve lights the mosquito coils, he warns his guest about the rat trap set on the narrow beam above. The trap is attached by a length of cord to the beam, Steve explains,

so there is no danger that a trapped rat will fall on the guest. But the guest should not be alarmed at hearing, in the dark, the death throes of a rat dangling above him.

The rats usually avoid the traps. All night long they thunder across the corrugated metal roof. From the sound of it, the rats are huge, but of course the metal amplifies them. It takes a rat an incredibly short time to traverse the roof. The guest lies awake, speculating on the speed of rats. He wonders whether the scratching of a rat's toenails on a metal roof is a disagreeable sensation to it. Or does the rat derive some sort of pleasure from that?

But the house where Bob Thomas lives alone is spare. Just as at work, where Thomas has everything at his fingertips, and can go straight to the map or blueprint drawer that he wants, so it is at home, except that here less needs organizing. In their simplicity his two small rooms have the illusion of space. The walls of the front room are entirely of fine-mesh screening, to let in the breeze. At intervals the screening is nailed to the 2 x 4 posts that support the corrugated roof. Thomas has rigged plywood shutters that can be lowered like drawbridges to cover the screens when it rains, but these are only on the seaward side of the house, the side from which the weather comes. The back room, where Thomas eats, sleeps, and washes under an improvised shower, has walls of corrugated metal and is always darker than the front.

The front room has a small plywood table. The table has a chair. On the floor are three Japanese glass fishing floats—small ones, about the size of softballs. There is no other furniture or decoration.

The back room has several shelves, on which coffee cups, cans of food, and other small items rest. Thomas's sleeping mat is rolled up and stored, along with his few possessions of any bulk, in one corner under another mat. On the walls are two faded Gauguin prints of Tahitian women, and several newspaper photos of statuary, cut from back pages and glued to squares of composition board. "The prayer." "The kiss." "Torment." And that is all. Rats would be wasting their time on his shelves.

Thomas writes for a while in his notebook. The notebook is large and black, filled with letters to himself, sketches, and architectural ideas. The sketches—mostly of flowers, palms, and thatch houses—are not particularly good. The ideas for structures are drawn more skillfully. Thomas is a calligrapher. In his drawings of schools, community centers, and bridges, the formula noted beneath is part of the composition. Sometimes the formulae are accompanied by warnings. They remind him of tidal peculiarities, or of a tendency toward formation of sand bars, that must be accommodated in building a bridge, and call his attention to other problems of the same sort. Here and there in his margins Thomas, the calligrapher, has sketched a numeral, or letter, of a style he has seen and liked.

Tamag's wife enters with a plate of rice and canned tuna, and Thomas puts his notebook aside. He accepts the plate. He would have preferred fresh fish, but no one in the village has been fishing today, apparently. The Yapese don't mind canned tuna. Canned fish, because it is rarer, is more interesting to them. Thomas does not seem to care much about food, and he doesn't mind either. He eats.

The breeze comes cool through the screening. When the sunset has flared, then subsided, and the light begins to die in the sky beyond the palms, and dies shortly afterward on the ocean, the wind seems to come up. The wind's whispering among the palm fronds rises. Why? At evening, when the heat of the day lessens, do tropical air masses begin to move differently? Or is it that with twilight, when eyes have less to see, ears switch on? Is the wind rising in the mind, or among the fronds, and how could you tell? (The wind rises suddenly, which seems to argue for the mind.) The light dies a bit more. A toad, barely discernible now, hops toward Tamag's cookhouse. From behind the house comes the regular quiet grunting of a pig. The pig seems to be talking to itself, making a mild complaint.

Then it's dark. The wind is in the palms still, but quieter. A male frog begins to announce his presence. The sound is like a very fast woodpecker on a thin, hollow log. From the direction of the cookhouse come the husky, serious voices of children. Then a step sounds on the road below. Someone—a man—passes and the road is silent again.

Robert Thomas, sitting on the floor in the light of his lantern, recites the Japanese that Tamag has been teaching him. His legs are folded under him in the yoga position assumed so easily by the people of countries without chairs. He speaks softly, but his voice is full of pleasure at what he's doing.

Often, for Peace Corps volunteers, the homesickness, and asceticism, and essential solitude of life in a strange land, causes the self to feel itself, and soar, in a melancholy way. The volunteer feels a little tragic. The feeling is not so deep, usually, that it can't be laughed at. Yet it is deep enough to be painful and precious. If anything characterizes Peace Corpsmen, everywhere, it is this pensive elevation. It is the feeling that Mike was flirting with, on his unknown birthday at O'Keefe's. For Robert Thomas,

the feeling seems to search for itself in his relation to Tamag. Thomas can't explain the relationship. He tries, but gives up almost instantly. He doesn't understand it himself. Tamag is there for him, not precisely as father nor as friend. It has to do somehow with the vast regions within each man that are forever secret to the other—their lives so different—yet in the understandings they share in spite of that. Seated on his barren floor, Thomas recites, like a monk his litany, the lesson Tamag has given him. In the night he sounds like a man who has read to his children to make them sleep, succeeded too soon at that, and is continuing now for himself.

Suddenly the quiet is startled by a shout, and from that commencement a male chant swells, filling the night. The sound is wild and full-throated and strange. Across the street the men of the village have begun practice for a coming dance. The singing is paced by the clapping of hands down a long line of seated men. The chant's sudden fullness and power is of the sort that makes tears jump to eyes, before the mind knows quite what is happening, as with certain hymns before prayer in black American churches. The sound threatens to carry Thomas's house away, yet Thomas does not falter in his recitation. The village men have been practicing for a week, so their abrupt commencement has not startled him. He is acquainted with all the men who make the sound. He has encompassed the strangeness, and he no longer hears it. He recites the Japanese, his inflection rising imperceptibly, as if to a far-distant climax.

After a time the singers cease, and go home. Thomas continues a while longer, then extinguishes his lantern.

In the morning, Thomas leaves for work before the sun is up. The house is empty when the first rooster crows. Then, with earliest light, roosters cry from several quarters, and soon from all around. The sun strikes the highest palm fronds, and moves downward. Soon the tops of all the slender, leaning trunks that line the road stand in young sunlight. The sun shines through a breadfruit leaf, dead and golden, that has blown up against the window screen. It strikes the plywood floor, and moves across it. From the cookhouse come women's voices. The women quickly warm to their conversation, and the Yapese syllables flow very fast. The name "Tamag" recurs several times. The accent is on the second syllable. This morning, in the women's mouths, the name sounds exactly like the Spanish *Tomás*. Spanish missionaries were the first Europeans here, a century ago. Surely "Tamag" is a corruption of the Spanish. Tamag and Thomas have the same name.

Out on the floating dock, Doublecheck has been work-

ing since first light. The ship leaves today. The Yapese longshoremen have taken much longer to load the cargo than they should have, and the Captain plans to sail whether or not the cargo is all aboard. By ten in the morning an army of Yapese longshoremen is present on the floating dock, but few are working at any one time. There are longshoremen of all ages, boys of twelve, their fathers and grandfathers. Most wear *thus*. They take frequent breaks, from work and from their conversations, to drink. On the deck stands a fifty-gallon drum of powdered milk, very dilute, sweetened with sugar, and around that they gather. They sip from the dipper, or from empty tin cans. The Yapese don't sail on schedules, and the Captain's problem is not very real to them. Only Doublecheck works without stopping. He is all business. He drives the forklift with great speed and efficiency. He works shirtless, under a crownless straw hat. Now, when Doublecheck is without his shirt, it is possible to see that his upper right arm is slightly deformed. It appears that the bone was broken once and set incorrectly. The arm does not slow him, and he labors without rest—working out

his own problem, surely, and not the Captain's.

By afternoon the cargo is loaded. The ship casts off from the loading dock, and makes her way slowly through the greenish waters of the channel. Past the fringing reef, she picks up speed. Yap falls behind. From the rail the young Chamorros watch the island recede. Their faces have fallen several nautical miles. They look like boys who have lost their mothers. Their connection on Yap did not come through, and they are without marijuana. Only Ben can manage a smile. Phillipe, who is sixteen and lied about this age to sign on the ship, stares down at the sea. At O'Keefe's Phillipe drank orange pop instead of beer—beer makes him sick—and yet, or because, he is of all the Chamorros the most dedicated to weed. He shakes his head tragically, as if it were pivoting under the weight of the world. Ben tries to cheer his comrades. There is said to be marijuana in Palau, he says. That's two days away. If not, there is certain to be some in the Philippines, five days beyond Palau. That's ten days or so, counting the layover in Palau. Ten days, he reminds them, is not forever.

6. PALAU AND BEYOND

ON THE Palauan island of Babeldaob there is a region called Ngchesar, from the interior of which runs the river Ngersuul. Like most tidal rivers, the Ngersuul is serpentine, twisting back on itself again and again, as if reluctant to meet the sea. But the river does meet the sea, in the end, and its brackish waters mingle with the salt of the lagoon. Singer Kochi turns his boat off the lagoon, enters the broad mouth of the Ngersuul, and steers upriver against the ebb tide. Kochi is conservation officer for the Palau Islands and he is looking for poachers.

Kochi is a big man, but not tall. He is strong enough to be the long-ball hitter on the Palauan baseball team, and quick enough to have been the ping-pong champion of Palau. These are credentials more impressive than they may seem, for Palau is an archipelago of athletes, and the competition there is rough. Kochi is thirty-three. He is an exuberant diver and fisherman, and a wildly boastful companion, among his American acquaintances, at least. Among Palauans boastfulness is not a virtue. Kochi is half Japanese, and started life with a much lighter complexion than his present dark brown. He has spent most of his life on the water, in the sun, where he earned his color. That he is here to navigate the Ngersuul at all is a minor miracle. He lived a violent and Spartan youth, in which he speared a number of childhood acquaintances and once tried to spear a teacher, but somehow he avoided jail. He attended high school in Guam, dropped out to join the Army, and then, after the cold of Korean winter, and race prejudice in Georgia, and the cities of Germany, and Army baseball in Japan, he came home to Palau. His was the sort of odyssey that few Micronesians return from, but Kochi found his way back.

The Japanese half of Kochi's ancestry is apparent mostly in his brows. They knit in a Samurai frown when he looks into the sun, or when, as in the pursuit of poachers, he is angry. In his war with poachers Kochi is implacable, and more than a little terrible. Palau's conservation laws are his Old Testament. He enforces them to the letter. Once he brought charges against Palau's marine conservationist, who was taking undersized turtles for an experiment, and another time he confiscated a rifle from his own brother, an unusual action in Palau, where officials commonly overlook the misdemeanors of members of their family or clan. Kochi is ingenious at devising methods for catching the pigeon poachers and fish dynamiters of his islands. He has had to be, for he is the single conservation enforcement officer for Palau's 188 square miles of jungle and savannah, her countless islands, islets, and her leagues of reef. And yet, for all his dedication, Kochi does not enjoy arresting people. His purpose is to stop poaching. When it's possible, he prefers to make himself conspicuous in a region, warning the people by his presence that a rifle shot, or the detonation of a fish bomb, would be a mistake. He travels about Palau constantly, working hard to achieve ubiquity, or a reputation for it.

The Ngersuul rapidly becomes narrower, once Kochi is within its mouth, so he slows down. At first the river is winding and mangrove bordered, like any other tidal river in the tropics. Besides water and sky there is nothing to see but the several species of mangrove, all very much alike. A white band on the bases of the dark, wet mangrove stilts marks how far the river has fallen since high tide. But soon, as Kochi follows the river's turnings inland, other trees begin to appear among the mangroves. He proceeds more slowly still, standing at the wheel and peering down into the brown water for snags. First pandanus, then trunkless nipah palms, the fronds of which grow straight from the wet soil, and then tree ferns appear by the riverside. After several river turns, it is the mangroves that are rare, and then they are gone. The Ngersuul becomes a jungle river. The boles of the trees now are huge, and the trunks bearded with epiphytes. In places the canopy overspreads the river. Vines the size of cables, whorled like the Bryozoan Archimedes, or like giant screws, dangle over the water. Kochi must duck to avoid them, yet keep up his watch for snags.

He dips his hand in the water, and tastes his fingers. The river is almost fresh. There is just a hint of brackishness, though the sea is still very near. The Ngersuul, then, is less a tidal river than it seems. Clearly a great volume of fresh water is flowing from the interior of Babeldaob—the second largest of Micronesia's islands—and out to sea. He dips again, this time to drink. In the river is a true taste of the island's size, for no small watershed could send down so much fresh. The taste makes the island's size real, in a way that no map could.

Kochi's propeller strikes a snag, and the motor shifts to its high injured pitch. Then the motor subsides. Kochi continues, watching more carefully now.

In Micronesia, where most islands are too small even for a stream, and most islanders draw their water from wells, a river seems rare and bounteous and not quite natural. It seems a special dispensation. The Ngersuul hints at deep and secret springs, and its mystery is in that, not in its mightiness, like the Mississippi, or in the way it flows through the history of the people, like the Ganges or the Nile, nor in its distant sources. It is not weighted with a lot of history, human or geological, and it seems a newer river. It flows as if from a rock recently cleft. Kochi is caught up in the spirit of its waters. Each new turn of the river calls him on, though the likelihood of poachers diminishes with each. As it rounds one turn, the boat's prow intersects the radiating ripples from something large that has just sunk. Singer Kochi, who always looks for the best, decides that this something was a crocodile. When he returns from patrol he will surely report seeing a crocodile. And in fairness, it *is* hard to imagine what other Palauan creature could have made

such a broad circle on the Ngersuul. As the boat passes the spot, Kochi peers deeply into the water.

Near the limit of navigation by outboard motor, the Ngersuul divides into two branches. Kochi chooses the righthand branch. It is not until he passes the mouth of the left that its shore discloses a boat, tied close to the bank. "Poachers," he thinks. He turns his boat around, enters the left-branching stream, cuts his motor, and poles up alongside the strange boat. He listens for gunshots. There are none. He shouts, but no one answers. Then, looking about, he sees a clearing above the riverbank. The clearing is planted to giant taro. So it's farmers then, not poachers. Kochi is pleased at finding the place. He had not known about it.

Meanwhile, south of Babeldaob, on the island of Koror, where Kochi lives and will soon return, the four Chamorros from the *Hoi Kung* are failing to buy marijuana. There was a Peace Corps Volunteer who grew a patch, they are told, but it was discovered, and he was shipped out. There isn't any on the island.

A week later the Chamorros fail also in the Philippines. They are desolate. Who could have predicted it? Who would have thought that no marijuana would be for sale in the Philippines, where you can buy girls, or for $75 buy a revolver stamped "Made in U.S.A."—a fair imitation of a model that, had it actually been made in the States, and were it sold there, would cost $60. In Micronesia, guns are rigidly controlled, and young Micronesian sailors jump at the chance to buy them in the Philippines. The imitation gun usually blows up the first time the Micronesian shoots it.

So the Chamorros are without marijuana as the ship leaves Davao and sails southward along the coast of Mindanao. They have had no opportunity as yet to shoot their guns, so the guns are tucked away, to be exploded at a later date. The Chamorros spend the morning painting the ship, and glancing from time to time at Mindanao's distant headlands, which slide slowly past. The sun is bright on the water and the Sulu Sea is spread out blue before them. They cover chipped or rusty spots in the ship's original white coat with circles and rectangles of green. There is no white paint available. Green spots dance before them, as if their eyes were shut for relief from the sun's scintillation. The radio rests on a coil of tarry hawsers, and the Chamorros work to its music. James Brown is singing. He comes through loud and clear on Radio Zamboanga. American music is impossible to escape, even in the middle of the Sulu Sea. Not that the

Chamorros want to escape it. As he paints, Ben tells an older sailor about Jimmy's Place in Sasa, and about El Cairo in Davao. Jimmy's is great, Ben says, but his eyes are without much enthusiasm, and don't agree. At Jimmy's you can get a girl for the whole night for 90 pesos, he says. That's about $15. The figure impresses him, in a gloomy way. The girls were nice girls who took showers when you told them to. "I feel sorry for them," Ben says. "It's the only way they can live. It's not too good." He looks young and cannabisless and far from home.

For the Chamorros the last desperate hope is Borneo. They know nothing about the place, but there is always the chance that marijuana grows there. In Borneo, unfortunately, the ship never reaches a town. After sailing part way up the Rejang River, it anchors in midstream. The cargo, hardwood from forests of the interior, is loaded from barges. The Chinese and Malay longshoremen are difficult to talk to. They live in wooden riverboats that cluster around the ship, and they come aboard only to cook their rice and shrimp over wood fires on the *Hoi Kung*'s deck. They speak little English, and no Chamorro at all. The Chamorros have trouble learning whether there is a town nearby, or any towns at all in Borneo. They are marooned in the middle of the river.

The Rejang is a broad tidal stream, with shores miles apart. Borneo is the third-largest island on the Earth, and its rivers have continental dimensions. The delta that the river twists through is endless, like a plain of reeds, except that here the reeds are nipah palms, with some mangroves mixed in. The mangroves are of unfamiliar varieties, and even the nipahs look different from Micronesia's. It is now clear, as it was not in the Philippines, that the ship has left the small islands of the Pacific behind. The wide, silty river conveys the weight of an eroding continent. It low banks are not sandy, as they would be in Micronesia, but are made of dark mud washed down from a distant mainland. When boats pass near the shore, lungfish with goggle eyes skip over the mud in large numbers, back into the protection of the water. It is mud of a sort that something might evolve from yet. Micronesia's sandy soils are innocent of that. The soil there is best at receiving colonizing seeds from some place else. So, for the Chamorros, home is behind them.

The sky above the nipah plain is as vast as the ocean sky. It is so broad that at a given time, in different quarters, six or seven ospreys can be seen hunting in it. The Chamorros' hearts might have lifted with the birds, but they do not, because of the prospect now before them. There will be no marijuana to break the monotony of the long haul back across the Pacific, all the way to California, with no ports to stop at, nothing to do but watch their ocean passing. In the old days, such would have been the makings of an epic voyage; heroic, and anything but boring. There were countless things to read in the passing waters then, but for the Chamorros now nothing is writ there, nothing legible, and the long, sunbleached, Homeric days will pass like blank pages.

Lines from Micronesian Classrooms

People of Micronesia have been for years trying to find the best type of government for Micronesia. As for my own opinion, I would like for Micronesia to become an independent nation. Although I know that this will be hard, I'd rather be under a government that it is run by a Micronesian than a foreigner. Even if my Micronesian leaders are like hell, I don't care. I don't like or want Micronesia to be under a foreign country.

—Justina Riklon

When I look outside I see a stupid caterpillar tractor and a man who drives it without mind, also a big dumping truck parking near the library. The big machine roars very loudly and it makes me feel sick and angry. There's some people standing at the M.O.C. building watching the caterpillar when it works. I think they surely like the sound of the big yellow machine.
I can see some of them laughing and pointing to something.

Well, good for them.

—Toribiong Masang

Poverty is trying to live as the Americans taught you.
Poverty is dressed with creases on your worn trousers, faded and mended shirt on your back.
Poverty is seeing them live comfortable, in concrete houses.
Poverty is seeing mowed lawns with gay colored flowers, overgrown grass in my yard instead.
And Poverty is when you are face to face sitting down at the table, mumbling "Bless us O Lord, and these thy gifts."

—Gonzalo Santo

My eyes see all things in the world—yet, have never seen the things I want.

—Caleb Darou

Many things have changed
when I saw the sunshine come
through the world this morning.

Sunshine makes the plants feel better.

The sunshine is a dryer.

Sunshine can give us a kind of love disease
when we see the sunset.

Sunshine is important to a place
where the people are playing.

Sunshine will be shone
and the white sand
will be brushed by the sea.

Look out to see the sunshine!
—PALAU HIGH SCHOOL

Insects buzz around
the flowers as if asking
flowers some questions.
—Lorinda Wenty

Trees are swaying outside.
  Rain is falling very hard
and children are
  chattering inside.
                    —ANON.

The last few days, there was windy nights. At my village there was a great
strong wind and rain. These caused the damage in the village. The wind blew
the banana trees and some tall trees. The wind wasn't strong enough to break
the roof out. I slept and thought about the wind that night. I thought
this wind caused the typhoon but this wind lasted only a few hours and
there was nothing at that time about typhoon. My mother was very afraid
of the great wind, so she slept but she never closed her eyes.

   One day when I was at the Rock Island and the wind became strong, I was
afraid. I was afraid because I thought that this hard wind would make the
danger of high water. And when the hard wind had gone it was quiet on the
island. The birds were flying in the air and singing and I started to feel
the breeze blowing on me, so I felt in love with the wind.
                    —BALTZAR

I stood and watched the sun set so it went down the horizon. When the sun
went down the sky turned into different kinds of color like the rainbow.
It made me so lonely when I watched all different colors appear in the sky
many ideas appeared in my head like I was dreaming and floating like a leaf
on the sea. I dreamed all the things I did in the past.

   I felt the cold air from the sea all around me so I remembered that I
was still standing on the same place. I turned and looked at the sky
the sky turned its color and became dark so I went home.

—ALICE THEL

In this great universe,
There is this tiny world
Among the big stars.
It is where life exists.
It is where we live.
—Stanley Heine

Have you every tried to sit in a secluded place and think about nature, the world around you with its countries and their different environments, different sceneries—how the plants pop up one after another without anyone's support for growth—the people with different faces; handsome, ugly, smart, ignorant, etc.?

If you haven't you may be abnormal. If you'll just take about half an hour and think of these things you'll realize that no human being can make such things. Then you will find yourself close to God. You will think of praying and giving thanks for the varied life we have.

—CHIRIKAR UEDA

On the reef with waves
The sun's shining on the sea.
How can I say no?
—MARIA MERSAI

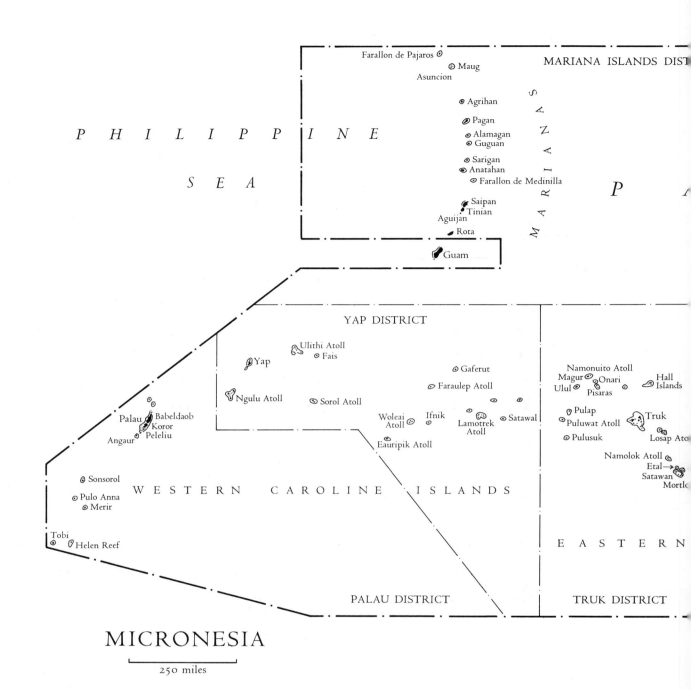

MICRONESIA

250 miles

FRIENDS OF THE EARTH

In its first four years, FOE has become one of the major U.S. conservation organizations. It has advocated the rights of nature before the three U.S. branches of government in testimony and in print, and has expedited the same environmental concern abroad through newly formed sister organizations, each adapting the same broad goal to its particular country's ways of doing things. FOE has undertaken substantial legislative activity and is not tax-deductible.

FOE has also gone deeply into several projects not legislative in character that were therefore eligible for financing with tax-deductible funds. It is important to know that such funds can now be made available through the Friends of the Earth Foundation, which receives them and provides donors with assurance that IRS regulations will be followed in their expenditure.

The Foundation, like FOE, believes its role must reach far beyond national boundaries, that environmental research and publishing can be most effective if conducted in many lands and languages by the people who live there and speak the languages.

Publisher's Note: The book is set in Centaur and Arrighi by Mackenzie & Harris Inc., San Francisco. It was lithographed and bound by Arnoldo Mondadori Editore, Verona, on coated paper made by Cartiera Celdit and Bamberger Kaliko Fabrik. The layout is by Kenneth Brower. The design is by David Brower.

FOE, 529 Commercial Street, San Francisco 94111

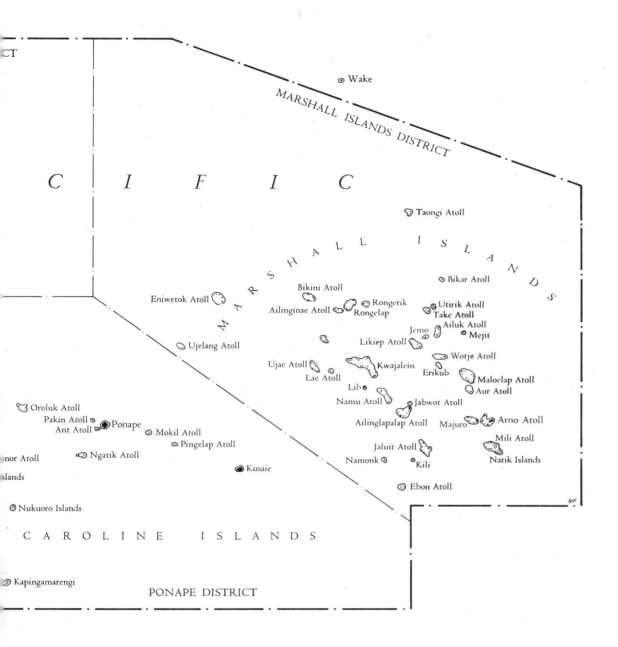

CT

⊘ Wake

MARSHALL ISLANDS DISTRICT

C I F I C

🦑 Taongi Atoll

M A R S H A L L   I S L A N D S

⊙ Bikar Atoll

Eniwetok Atoll 🦪   Bikini Atoll 🦪
                Ailinginae Atoll 🦪 🦪 Rongerik   ⊙ Utirik Atoll
                          Rongelap   Take Atoll
                                            Ailuk Atoll
                                      Jemo 🦪   ⊙ Mejit
⊙ Ujelang Atoll   Likiep Atoll 🦪
                Ujae Atoll 🦪   🦪 Kwajalein   🦪 Wotje Atoll
                  Lae Atoll 🦪   Erikub 🦪
                          Lib 🦪   🦪 Maloelap Atoll
🦑 Oroluk Atoll   Namu Atoll 🦪   🦪 Aur Atoll
Pakin Atoll 🦪 🦑 Ponape   🦪 Jabwot Atoll
Ant Atoll ⊙ Mokil Atoll   Ailinglapalap Atoll 🦪 Majuro 🦪 Arno Atoll
          ⊙ Pingelap Atoll   Mili Atoll
nor Atoll 🦪 Ngatik Atoll   Jaluit Atoll 🦪   🦪
slands   🦑 Kusaie   Namonk ⊙ ⊙ Kili   Narik Islands

⊙ Nukuoro Islands   ⊙ Ebon Atoll   NF

C A R O L I N E   I S L A N D S

🦑 Kapingamarengi   PONAPE DISTRICT

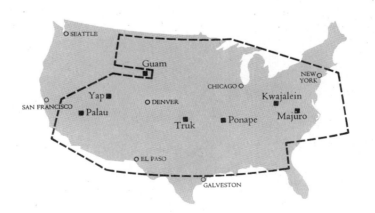

Breakers, Marshalls